SHIFT
HAPPENS!

Also by Robert Holden, Ph.D.

Happiness NOW!

Hello Happiness

Balancing Work & Life (with Ben Renshaw)

Success Intelligence

SHIFT HAPPENS!

Powerful Ways to Transform Your Life

ROBERT HOLDEN, Ph.D.

Jeffers
press

Santa Monica, California

A Jeffers Press Book
Copyright © 2000 by Robert Holden
First Jeffers Press edition published 2006

Published in the United States and Canada by Jeffers Press, a division of Susan Jeffers, LLC, P.O. Box 5338, Santa Monica, California 90409. First published in Great Britain in 2000 by Hodder and Stoughton, a division of Hodder Headline

www.jefferspress.com
ISBN 10: 0-9777618-2-7
ISBN 13: 978-0-9777618-2-1

Publisher's Cataloging-in-Publication
(*Provided by Quality Books, Inc.*)

Holden, Robert, 1965-
　　Shift happens : powerful ways to transform your life
/ Robert Holden. -- 1st Jeffers Press ed.
　　p. cm.
　　Includes bibliographical references.
　　ISBN-13: 978-0-9777618-2-1
　　ISBN-10: 0-9777618-2-7

　　1. Self-actualization (Psychology)　I. Title.

BF637.S4H643 2006　　　　　158.1
　　　　　　　　　　　　　QBI06-600315

Cover and text design by Dotti Albertine

Printed in the USA

*I dedicate
this book to the
Unconditioned Self
in each of us.*

ACKNOWLEDGMENTS

Gratitude is a gift because it helps you see how many gifts you have been given. Thank you to everyone for all the gifts I have received in writing this book. Thank you to Miranda for her vision, wisdom and midnight snacks! Thank you to my family and friends for their love. Thank you to my family at The Happiness Project. Thank you to Candy Constable for her "make it so" skill. Thank you to Ben Renshaw for his total dedication to joy. Thank you to my editor Rowena Webb for her support.

One of the greatest gifts of my life is a book called *A Course in Miracles.* I acknowledge both author and scribe for their great gift of love. Thank You. This book is a miracle.

NOTE: Every case history in this book appears with the consent of those involved. Names have been altered where requested.

CONTENTS

CONTENTS

CONTENTS

INTRODUCTION

Two caterpillars were crawling along a tree branch one day when a butterfly flew overhead. One caterpillar said to the other, *"You will never get me up in one of those things."*

Shift Happens! is about personal alchemy and inner transformation. *Some people "go" through life; and other people "grow" through life.* *Shift Happens!* celebrates your unlimited potential to grow, blossom and evolve—in spite of everything. It is a book of hope.

The term *personal alchemy* describes the ability to take a piece of dirt, roll it around a few times, and fashion it into a pearl. This is what an oyster does. Personal alchemy is what your grandmother called turning lemons into lemonade. It is what old wizards described as turning straw into gold.

Shift Happens! is about staying open all hours for miracles. Success, love and happiness are only ever one thought away at most. One new perception, one fresh thought, one act of surrender, one change of heart, one leap of faith, can change your life forever.

HAPPINESS IS AN INNER LIGHT WITH NO "OFF" SWITCH

Dublin is a beautiful city. I am often invited to speak there. One year, I shared a platform with Dr. Deepak Chopra, the renowned spiritual teacher and author. We had a thousand people packed into the hall that day. I began with a talk entitled *From Hell to Happiness: A One-way Ticket.* I think I was about twenty minutes into my talk when I first heard an odd gurgling sound. As I searched for where the sound was coming from, I noticed a young mother and her small baby sitting near the front. It was the baby who was gurgling, and quite musically too!

Now, I want you to know that I thought my talk was going quite well. I was espousing beautiful, sacred principles of truth that were undoubtedly insightful, enlightening, very wise and a joy to behold! However, it was soon clear to me that this little baby had an audience. The musical gurgling had grown louder and was now echoing all the way down the hall. I graciously gave way.

"Excuse me," I said, addressing the young mother. "How old is your child?"

"Ten weeks old," she replied.

"Girl or boy?"

"Boy."

He looked absolutely beautiful. Everyone was now straining their necks to take a look. "Would you mind standing up so everyone can see your beautiful baby?" I asked. The young mother did so without hesitation. And one thousand people sang out "Ahhh!" in perfect unison. We all melted. And then, guess what? One thousand people started clapping. And cheering!

When the ovation finally died down and the mother returned to her seat with her child, I was left to get on with my crummy old talk. A thought then occurred to me that I put to my audience. "Do you realize," I said, "that if this young mother had held up a forty-year-old man or woman no one would have gone "Ahhh!" and certainly no one would have clapped and cheered?" The laughter that followed made my point.

What exactly had this baby done to earn such a tumultuous ovation of love and positive regard? Surely it had nothing to do with IQ, academic excellence, resume, business acumen or financial status! He couldn't kick a football, he was no actor, and he was too young to have his own chat show. All he did was sleep, gurgle, dribble and pass wind. Adults tend not to get ovations for that sort of stuff.

I believe this young baby reminded us of something about ourselves. He was a symbol for our Unconditioned Self. This Unconditioned Self is the real "you". It is the essential you that outlives the body. It is the "real you" that promised to be the presence of love, the light of the world, and God's angel on earth.

Your Unconditioned Self is your original potential. It is the memory of God that you forget about as you grow up and *stuff happens,* i.e., bumps, bruises, school grades, puberty, heartbreaks, job interviews, rejections, parking tickets, the rat race, traffic, the mortgage, a pension, etc.

Since time began, the wise ones in every culture have carried a torch for the Unconditioned Self. This Self is like an inner light with no "off " switch. You may lose sight of it, but it never goes out. Zen masters called this Unconditioned Self your *original face*; Taoists, the *uncarved block; Christians, your *original innocence*; Hindus, *eternal bliss consciousness;*

Alchemists, your *inner gold*; St Francis of Assisi, your *eternal loveliness*; Thomas Merton, your *secret beauty*. And so on.

It is your lack of faith in your Unconditioned Self, i.e., your inner light, that leads you into dark places and dark stories. Every time you betray your original power and innocence you participate in illusions of separation, struggle, smallness, fear and unworthiness. Shift happens when you consciously reconnect to your wisdom and your light. This is what true healing is about.

Remember today that *happiness is not an it!* Happiness is not in things; it is in you. Happiness is your inner light that has no "off" switch. Be still for a moment. Stop the world. Close your eyes. Sink into your heart. Let every in-breath be a symbol of your intention to connect unconditionally to love, life and joy. And let every out-breath be a symbol of your willingness to let go of separation and fear.

Do this until you touch something infinite. Your soul. All the angels will applaud. And guess what? They will cheer too!

YOU ARE WHAT YOU SEEK!

I first met Susan in a mental health hospital in London. Susan was a lawyer, thirty-something, tall, with dark hair and olive skin, attractive, witty, intelligent, and very depressed. This was her fourth time as an inpatient. She was diagnosed with chronic resistant depression.

Susan was sitting in the patients' lounge. She was playing with a jigsaw puzzle. I said "Hello" and asked her how she was getting on.

"Okay," she said.

"It looks like you have nearly finished the puzzle," I said.

"Yeah, but I probably won't get to finish it," replied Susan.

"Why not?"

"Well, I suspect there may be a piece missing."

I saw Susan again at the end of my visit. She was reading a magazine.

"Did you finish the puzzle?" I asked.

"Yeah," she replied.

"What about the missing piece?" I asked.

"Everything was here," she smiled.

"Great!"

"Yeah, I always think there must be a piece missing. It's the story of my life," she said. We both smiled because we both knew what she was talking about.

The fear that something is missing somewhere in you or in your life is the greatest illusion of all. It is a rogue thought that can wreak havoc with perception, creating much self-doubt, self-criticism and self-attack. It is a dastardly magician that conjures up mental tricks of lack, loss, isolation, neediness, dependency and much pain.

The fear that something is missing in you is what leads you to search *somewhere else* for happiness. You overlook what is already "here" as you chase after "there"; you miss the "sacred now" as you ponder your "next step"; you forget to be grateful for what "is" as you prey after "more". You search, struggle and strive, but you never arrive because you can't get past the thought that something is missing.

Can you see that all your pain comes from the belief that your source of happiness is outside you? This single misperception—this little fear—is what feeds your mental junk, your learned unworthiness, and your "not good enough" stuff. Notice how all thoughts of fear and lack are reversed the moment you accept that every piece of universal joy rests already in your heart. Feel this, now.

Every culture has its sacred sites and holy meeting grounds. Thousands of people every day travel in pilgrimage to far off places like Lourdes, the Great Pyramids, Ayers Rock, the Grand Canyon, Mount Shasta, Stonehenge, Mount Athos, the Himalayas. These places hold sacred energy, they say. And yet, nowhere is more sacred than the human heart—home of your Unconditioned Self. *You are sacred ground.* Do you see this?

Your two physical eyes see bits of things. They see bits of the color spectrum, bits of the landscape, bits of the ocean, bits of the sky. They see bits of you and bits of me. But they do not see the big picture. It is only when you look with the heart that you can begin to comprehend the possibility of true wholeness, true beauty and true oneness.

It is my experience that the most amazing people act as if everything is already here. Great artists tune in to something universal when they create. Great thinkers trust in a solution for every problem. Great leaders lend themselves to constant guidance and inspiration. Great healers see people's wholeness long before any cure arrives.

Imagine that! Imagine whatever you want is here right now. What do you want? Wisdom? It's already here. Peace? It's already here. Inspiration? It's already here. It's all here, because you are. This is the big picture. This is what your Unconditioned Self sees.

You are what you seek. This means that whatever joy you hoped "to get" after you found your true partner, got the dream job, bought the ideal home and earned the right money is *already in you*! When you search for love, joy, power, money, heaven and God, you are really searching for the experience of your Unconditioned Self that is unencumbered by fear, separation and lack.

You are not here to find happiness; you are here to extend it. You are inspiration-packed, wisdom-infused, made with love and blessed with joy. And so is everyone else. To be free, all you have to do is make yourself wholly available to what is already inside you. Real healing is giving up your resistance to your Unconditioned Self.

Here is some *graffiti for the soul*. "I am everything I seek".

Write it down on a piece of paper and stick it in your wallet. Truth is here, inspiration is here, love is here, peace is here, help is here, God is here, because you are here. Truth is a pathless land, and happiness is a *journey without distance*.

THERE IS NOTHING WRONG WITH YOU

The following story describes one of the most poignant and tender moments of my life.

I met Peter at a summer camp for The Royal National Institute for the Blind in Hampshire, England. Peter was in my class. I was teaching a day on self-esteem to fifty teenagers. They were like any large group of teenagers in school—creative, unruly, funny, boisterous, challenging and very energetic. They were normal … and blind.

Peter was one of the few quiet ones. He sat at the back of the class. He was half-Chinese, half-English, about fifteen years old, tall and slender. There were many jokes flying around, most of them at my expense. Peter laughed heartily, but he never spoke. At the end of the class, he stayed behind. "Mr. Holden," he said.

"Call me Robert," I said.

"Can we talk?" he asked.

"Certainly," I replied.

Peter looked troubled. He was pensive and painfully shy.

24

We talked small-talk for a while as we lapped a large green sports field out behind the main college building. "I feel I can trust you Robert, even though we have only just met," he said.

"That's a real compliment," I said.

"I need to ask you a question that I have been putting off my whole life," Peter said.

I was in no way prepared for Peter's question when it finally came. "I need to know," he said, "is there anything wrong with me?"

"What do you mean?" I asked.

"I was born blind and I have never seen myself. I need to know from someone I trust if I am beautiful or not," Peter said.

With all my heart, I told Peter that he was handsome, perfect and beautiful.

"You really mean it?" he asked.

"Yes—totally."

Peter flung his arms around me. "There's nothing wrong with me?"

"No!"

"Not even a little bit wrong?"

"Not one bit."

"What about my breath—I had pizza for lunch," he laughed.

"I love garlic," I countered. We both laughed and cried. Rarely have I felt so moved. Peter's relief was a joy to watch.

For six years I trained in a profession that majors in finding things wrong with people. We take in "ugly ducklings" and merrily pluck away for disorders, dysfunctions, neuroses, psychoses, syndromes and schemas. Psychology is obsessed with diagnosis. Every day we invent new labels, new diseases and new courses of treatment for the "ugly ducklings". We never see them as swans.

The fear that something is wrong with you is your greatest block to joy. In truth, there is no other block.

For as long as you judge there is something wrong, bad, lacking or not good enough about you, your life will reflect this belief. On the face of it, it will look as though others reject you, the world blocks you, fate is unkind, life is against you, and the heavens are punishing you. But in fact, it is you who are condemning yourself and sabotaging all that is good. Hence everything is a struggle, successes are hard-fought, happiness is short-lived, love always goes wrong, and there is no peace.

There is nothing wrong with you. Certainly, your perception can be sick. And your thinking can be off. And you can make poor choices. For instance, you can choose to see flaws in yourself that no one else sees. You can invent a story of how bad you are. You can try to convince the world how unlovable you are. Give these strange ideas all your power, if you want, but *who you are—your Unconditioned Self*—remains whole, worthy and well.

True psychotherapy is a process of changing your mind about yourself. Shift happens whenever you practice *unconditional* self-acceptance. Shift happens whenever you give yourself a break. Shift happens whenever you choose kindness instead of judgment, forgiveness instead of self-attack, laughter instead of condemnation. Life always gets better when you treat yourself better.

Happiness is all about being willing to be innocent again. Remember that old bumper sticker, *God doesn't make junk!* It's true.

The final (and only) act of healing is to accept there is nothing wrong with you. Try this powerful exercise today. Make a point of looking for the good in everyone you meet. See the light in their eyes, their faces, their smile and their presence. Mentally bow to the light in everyone you meet today. Above all, teach no one that there is anything wrong with *who they are*. As you offer this light to others so will you strengthen it in yourself.

THAT WHICH SUFFERS IS NOT YOU

have watched both my parents suffer great pain. My father drank himself to death. For ten years he lived homeless on the streets. My mother has suffered deep depression. Twice she has tried to kill herself. I too know what it is to want to die. Everyone alive has been tempted to die at some very low point in life.

You know what it is to suffer. I do not need to meet you to know that. *You have felt like two-thirds of a Rice Krispie—you've snapped, you've crackled and you are about to pop!* You have felt pain. You have made mistakes. You have experienced failure. You have had illnesses. You have had a dark night of the soul. These experiences are like nightmares. Bad nightmares. **But they are not your identity.** They are not *who you are* or *what you are*. To think this would be a gross act of Self-denial.

To remain true to your Unconditioned Self, you must distinguish between experiences and identity. For instance, can you see the difference between saying, "I experienced failure" and "I am a failure"? Or, between saying, "I made a mistake" and "I'm stupid"? Certain Buddhist teachers would counsel you to say, "I am with fear" instead of "I am afraid". Why? Because *you* are not your suffering.

In psychology school I learned about illnesses, symptoms and problems, but not people. I could stick a label on anyone from a mile away, but what I could not see was the person behind the label. Psychology is full of anger specialists, stress consultants, anxiety therapists and depression experts, as medicine is full of experts in body parts, ailments and diseases. Physicians for the whole person are thin on the ground. A shift in focus is needed.

On graduation, I made a vow to treat people, not illnesses. To me, there are no alcoholics, no cancer patients, no anorexics, no AIDS victims, no neurotics, no psychotics. I will not define people by their illnesses. Every illness is a façade that hides the whole person. On the other side of every fearful thought there is wholeness. Your wholeness can be eclipsed, but never put out.

When you are in pain, it is your thoughts that suffer, not you. Pain is about fearful thoughts, dashed hopes, broken promises, crushed expectations, unmet demands, failed plans and shattered dreams. These are thoughts you identify with, but they are not you. It is your attachment to these thoughts that causes pain. Give up the attachment and you are free.

I have a card I sometimes give to my clients to help them remember that *you are not your suffering*. It reads:

> I am not an illness.
> My symptoms are not who I am.
> No single failure is my entire biography.
> Mistakes are moments, not nameplates.
> Pain is an experience, not an identity.
> That which suffers is not me.
> Thoughts are just thoughts.
> Fears are just fears.
> Pain is transient.
> The past is over.
> Wholeness.

Buddhists say that attachment is the source of all suffering in this world. This is especially true of attachment to suffering.

Whatever you identify with you attract more of. Thus, when you identify with suffering, you attract more suffering—not because you like it, but because it feels familiar. Even worse, the fear of wellness sets in. In other words, you are so attached to suffering there is no room at the inn for something beautiful, something new, something magnificent.

Shift happens when you let go of attachment to suffering. I have learned that problems are not fixed; they are simply outgrown. You leave them behind. Thus, to experience healing and wholeness you have to be willing to give up your attachment to the self ...

> that has made mistakes.
> that has experienced failure.
> that has suffered illnesses.
> that messed up.
> that has been abused.
> that was betrayed.
> that was once unpopular.
> that has been victimized.
> that grew up poor.

that was rejected.
that was wrongly accused.
that did not get the love.

A client of mine, Claire, had experienced Chronic Fatigue Syndrome (CFS) for over ten years. At first, her physicians told her the illness did not exist. Later, they confirmed it did and she was diagnosed with different "types" by different specialists. Finally, she was told there was no cure, only remission. That was when she came to see me, *to find herself again*.

Claire and I worked well together. Her remission was good! Several months passed before she called again. "Robert, I need your help one more time," she said. Claire had kept a daily diary of her CFS experience for almost eight years. She said, "You have taught me to honor my experience of this illness, *but not to give it my identity*. I want to give my diary away now. I want to move on with my new life."

After some more talking, Claire decided to burn the diary in her back garden. Together with her family, we created a ritual in which we honored her past experiences *and* committed to present joy and happiness. Letting go was harder than Claire had imagined. But now she was free.

Take time today to honor all your experiences. Smile, *and let each one go.* Your experiences are simply experiences. They are not you. Above all, you are not an illness, you are not made of pain, and you are not your mistakes. You are far too beautiful for that.

YOU CAN HAVE
WHATEVER YOU WANT

When I was twenty-five years old, I went to listen to a talk given by an Indian holy man who was touring Europe. I had not heard of this holy man before, but my interest had been strongly peaked by the outrageous title of his talk which was, "You can have whatever you want!"

The room was full of jasmine incense, beautiful orchids, Indian music, pictures of Krishna, statues of Ganesh (god of spiritual wealth), a bookstall, a table covered with fine cloths, and over two hundred people. I sat down on a small cushion. There were no chairs. The music died down. There was a short silence. The holy man entered. Everyone bowed.

The holy man smiled. He then began, "It is God's joy to give you everything. Know you can have whatever you want. Be still, and know who you are." Good start, I thought. That was, however, the end of the talk! The holy man's assistant then told us we would each receive an individual silent blessing called a Darshan. We were also told this is a rare gift.

One by one, the audience left their cushions to stand before the holy man. In complete silence, he first smiled and then looked directly into the eyes of the person before him. After thirty seconds or so he pressed his hand against the person's forehead. The assistant then handed out an Indian sweet and the silent blessing was complete. Each person was visibly moved.

There was a great stillness in the room by the time I went up to receive my Darshan. I felt nervous and self-conscious as I approached the holy man, but his big bronze face and big white smile quickly put me at ease. As he looked into my eyes, he said, "*Who are you?*"

I was shocked. He wasn't meant to speak. "I am Robert Holden," I said.

He smiled. "No. *Who are you?*"

My breath faltered. "I am a writer," I said.

He smiled again. "No. *Who are you?*"

I searched desperately for an answer he might like. "I am a soul," I said.

He chuckled to himself and again said, "*Who are you?*"

I had no words. There was nothing to say. I understood.

The holy man from India gave me a most precious gift that day. He asked me to look past my labels, my self-image, my learned self, and *who I think I am*, so as to see the truth of who I really am, i.e., my Unconditioned Self. With great compassion he encouraged me to win back all that is infinite, immeasurable and eternal.

Every moment of your life you are deciding, 1) *who you are*; 2) *what you want*; 3) *what you can do*; 4) *what you deserve, and don't*. In effect, you create a self-image, i.e., an opinion of yourself. Your self-image then creates your reality by underwriting what it deems is possible and not possible, i.e., your self-image contracts how much success you can have, how much happiness is "realistic", how much peace of mind is okay, how much love is acceptable, and how much abundance is possible.

You choose your self-image, and therefore you choose your life. Be careful then not to make up your mind about yourself (and others) too quickly. Do not be so quick to condemn yourself, to be conditioned, to wear a label, to pigeonhole your talents, to argue what is not possible, and to decide how life *must be*. Stay open and alive to new choices and new possibilities.

Relax for a moment. Be willing to let go of every "I am", i.e., I am a woman, I am a man, I am young, I am old, I am

American, I am African, I am a mother, I am a father, I am an accountant, I am an actor, I am not creative, I am not lucky, I am not loved, I am still searching, etc. Relax, let go, peel away and undo every little "I am" so as to reveal your true Unconditioned Self.

And do the same with every "I can't", i.e., "I can't find love", "I can't attract money", "I can't get the support", "I can't sing", "I can't give up smoking", "I can't find a job", "I can't let go", "I can't meditate", "I can't dance", "I can't read your mind", "I can't believe it", "I can't change", etc. Let every little "I can't" fly away like butterflies in a summer sky. In truth, there is no "I can't".

Put your self-image in the hands of heaven. Let the angels sing to you hymns of divinity. Give God your tiny self-image, so that God may show you your true beauty. Be unconditional. Be open to yourself. Be like the child who asked its mother, "Who am I?", and the mother responded, "You are so beautiful you can be whoever you want."

THERE IS NO SEPARATION

My great-uncle, Derek Hill, once invited me on a short stay to Tory Island, a remote little island off the coast of Donegal, Ireland. Derek is a gifted artist. His landscape portraits of this rugged, beautiful island live in many of the world's most famous art museums.

To get to Tory Island you have to travel on three boats. First, you climb into a small dinghy that takes you out to the main boat. Then, you travel for seven nautical miles at top speed through the mighty waves of the Atlantic. Finally, you jump into another small dinghy that takes you to the main shore of Tory Island. The whole trip takes about an hour and a half.

Approximately 150 people live on the island. There is one of everything there—one church, one hotel, one hall, one shop, one main road, one pub, one helicopter and one king. Yes—the island has its own king!

My uncle and I walked the entire island in less than an hour. First we went to the east coast. It was beautiful. Quiet.

Solitary. We met no one. We then went over to the west coast. Here we met three locals. They were very friendly and welcoming. I happened to mention that we did not meet anyone on the east side. "That would be right," they said, looking very grave. "You see, the people over there are all a bit strange."

Even here, on this tiny island, there was a cold war, an east–west divide!

Separation is the great illusion. Albert Einstein called it an optical delusion. Yasutani Roshi, the spiritual teacher, said, "The fundamental delusion of humanity is to suppose that I am here and you are out there." The truth is, you are not separate from anything, ever. There is no time and space between you and God. And you are never separate from life or from the subatomic unity that makes mountains, amethysts and stars.

Separation is the great disease of mankind. It is because you believe you are separate and alien to the rest of life that you experience lack, struggle, conflict, illness and pain. Think about it! It is impossible to feel wholly connected to life and be depressed. It is impossible to experience pure oneness and have anxiety. It is impossible to join unconditionally with someone and be in fear. It is impossible to be in God and in hell.

Separation is hell. When you are tempted to fence off a

piece of the whole and call it "self", "mine" and "own", the price you pay for these acquisitions is to feel estranged, separate and disassociated from the whole field of creation. Everything now feels outside "you", including happiness, love, peace, heaven and God. The word "hell" in old English means "fence" or "boundary".

Separation, by its very nature, is violent. The moment you believe you are separate from anything or anyone there is room for suspicion, fear, defensiveness, competitiveness, envy and attack. Because of separation, it is now you against the world, you against your neighbor, you against your brother, you against "them", you against God. And because you are too afraid to extend love to anything that is not "your own" you suffer even more.

Separation is like a cancer. In my work I have found that separation from your true Unconditioned Self plays a part in almost every illness and unhappiness. Separation from your innate wholeness can spread quickly, causing you to feel cut off from nature, from humanity, from your own feelings, from your creativity, from your higher self and from hope.

It is because *separation is the root of dis-ease and pain* that all healing begins with dropping your defenses, giving up your secrets, reaching out, asking for help, receiving, letting others in, being intimate, and joining.

If you are interested in having more energy, more inspiration, more creativity, more grace, more peace, more aliveness and more joy, all you have to do is give up the illusion of separateness. Begin each new day with this simple prayer: "*Dear God, today I give up the thought of separation. Amen.*" You are not separate. And you do not walk alone. Affirm to yourself daily:

> *In me is all of Heaven;*
> *In Heaven is all of me.*

DETOX YOUR EGO!

The ego is obviously not real. It has never been photographed or X-rayed. No autopsy has ever found an ego. No faxes, e-mails or photocopies of an ego exist anywhere. Clearly, *the ego is just an idea*. That being so, the short version of this chapter reads: "You are not your ego". The slightly longer version of this chapter now follows!

The ego is a "small idea". Indeed, it is the sum total of all your small ideas about yourself. Your ego sees you as separate, isolated and cut off from the whole. Your ego is, to quote Austin Powers, your "mini me". It is like a little finger puppet version of the real, immeasurable you. It is a blind spot that fails to see your infinite, unconditional Self.

The ego is a detour from wholeness to lack. "Look out!" is the ego's prayer. In my book, *"Happiness NOW!"* I describe the EGO as a belief that <u>E</u>verything <u>G</u>ood is <u>O</u>utside. Believe the ego and you must embark on a search for happiness outside you. Now you participate in the greatest illusion of all, for the search for happiness is really the denial of happiness.

The ego is made of fear. It fears you are alone, in exile from God. It fears you do not have what it takes to be successful and happy. It fears you are unworthy and unlovable. It fears you are not good enough for the good things in life. The ego is Self-doubt. It is the "mafia of the mind". It cannot see the big picture. Your ego is really a call for love.

The ego is a limited perspective of your true Unconditioned Self. It is your learned ideas about who you are, as opposed to God's unconditional truth about you. The following poem of mine, "What is the ego?", aims to illustrate the ego's "bit-part" perspective. It reads:

> The ego is one small stone on a landscape.
> It is a temporary ink stain on your face.
> The ego is your one and only mistake today.
> It is the dandruff on your collar.
> The ego is a piece of litter on an acre of land.
> It is a speck of dust in your palace.
> The ego is a single coffee granule in Brazil.
> It is one drop of paint on the artist's easel.
> The ego is the "i" in humanity.
> It is one note in the whole symphony.

The ego is one word in your dictionary.
It is one electron in electricity.
The ego is a bad joke.
It is the single calorie in your diet coke.
The ego is one flower in the whole garden.
It is one split pea in your split pea soup.
The ego is one light particle in the sky.
It is but one star in the whole universe.
The ego is one idea destined to die.
In truth, it is not you and it is not I.

The ego, being a thought of lack, resists the idea of unconditional joy. It cannot conceive of a "free lunch", of "no pain, all gain", or of simply surrendering to joy. According to your ego, happiness must always involve a pay policy, a plan, some justification, hard work and struggle. As such, the ego is all that stands before you and happiness now, love now, peace now, heaven now, inspiration now, God now.

Your ego will always try to sell you something you already have. The ego says you must "fill in the form". *Your life must look right before you can be happy.* Hence, to be happy you must first get the right job, the right friends, the right partner, the right money, the right clothes, the right figure, the right car, the right toupee, the right postcode, and you must get everything you do *right!* How exhausting is this?

What have you told yourself you must get right before self-acceptance, before happiness, before you can relax? The ego offers you happiness at the "right price". Your Unconditioned Self wants you to know happiness is a choice. What do you want? *Do you want to be right, or happy?*

Shift happens every time you detox your ego. Compassion, kindness, forgiveness and humor are good detox agents. Humor busts the ego. Anything else is just too serious. To try to control, kill or heal your ego only serves to make it more real than it is. Remember, your ego has no power other than what you give it.

Take a moment now to remind yourself: your happiness is like an inner light with no "off" switch; you are what you seek; there is nothing wrong with you; that which suffers is not you; there is no separation; and the more you love the more you get what you really want. Love and ego cannot co-exist. Love is wholeness. Love detoxifies the ego! Love dissolves what was never there.

BEWARE OF "I" STRAIN

There is a long heritage of fierce independence on my father's side of the family. My father's grandmother, for example, was blind for nine years before she told anyone. Like many truly independent people, she was "tough as nails" on the outside and all warm marshmallow on the inside.

My most abiding memory of my father's parents was the night of their Diamond Wedding anniversary. A huge feast was followed by a disco and dancing. It was great fun, even if we did have to listen to my grandmother's favorite song over and over again. This was Frank Sinatra's *My Way* —the ultimate anthem for any independent person.

My father carried the independent flag to his death. He was a bighearted loner. A self-made man. And all by himself, he drank himself to death. No help was good enough for him. The baton of independence was then passed to me, and I really ran with it. I was a self-starter. I was a complete one-man show. By my late twenties, I had written four books, founded two successful clinics, given over a thousand seminars, had my own radio show, and more. I was independent, successful ... and exhausted.

From a distance, the independent person cuts a striking pose. To be independent looks like power, freedom and true strength. But it isn't. Independence is not strength, it is a wound. Independence is inspired not by love, but fear, and not by wholeness, but aloneness. Independence is the ego's attempt to be its own god. It is a form of arrogance that leads to much despair. The independent person always runs out of juice.

How do you know if you are being *dysfunctionally independent*? Here are a few tell-tale signs:

- You are exhausted because "superman" and "super woman" insist on being self-sufficient.
- You never ask for help. You are too scared, proud, arrogant and anal to accept help.
- You get a "Fail" for receiving. You never let anyone give to you.
- You suffer from BMS—*By Myself Syndrome.* This is true of everything, even sex!
- Intimacy is unfamiliar and scary. It is impossible to be independent and intimate.

- You think being free is being single.
- You look cool, but that is because you are cut off from your feelings.
- You try to heal on your own. At best you use a meditation tape, but you would never open up to another person. You are taking self-help to an extreme.
- You are in competition with everyone because you will not join with anyone.
- Atheism is your revenge on God. You are disillusioned because God won't see it "my way."

Independence is unnatural and not clever. There are 6,000,000,000 people on the planet and you are trying to "do" life on your own! There are 6,000,000,000 people in your backyard and you say there is no one out there for you. There are 6,000,000,000 people here and you won't trust one person. There are 6,000,000,000 people and you believe people are lucky if they make one or two good friends in life.

Believing you have to be independent is the ego pulling the wool over your eyes. Independence is unnecessary and it does not work. Think about it! Even Robinson Crusoe had Friday.

Even the Lone Ranger had Tonto. Even Superman had Lois. And Batman had Robin, Bob had Bing, Fred had Ginger, Lennon had McCartney, Lloyd Webber had Rice, Jeeves had Wooster, Arthur had Merlin, Thelma had Louise, Fred had Barney. Got it?

So the key question is, when did you decide to become so independent? What are you afraid of? Who hurt you? Who let you down? When did you lose your faith? What are you defending against? Don't answer these questions on your own! That would be being dysfunctionally independent. Be open to some additional help and insight. Shift happens when you stop flying the flag of independence. You get your energy, your creativity and your life back.

There is a better way than independence. Give yourself some time today to make a list of your "team". By that I mean everyone and everything that may potentially be a source of strength and inspiration. People have talents, strengths and gifts you can't see yet because you are not asking for help. Just imagine, maybe all the universe is here to support you. Drop your cynicism. It is an old wound. Open up to life. Let people in. Let yourself be nourished and given to. This is true strength.

GOD DOES NOT BELIEVE IN ATHEISTS!

Peter was an eminent psychiatrist with his own independent practice who telephoned me out of the blue one day. "I have read your book *Happiness NOW!* and think you may be able to help me, Mr. Holden".

"How so?" I asked.

Peter's voice was full of emotion when he said, "I am in a hole. A big hole. I have tried everything I know, but I just can't think my way out."

Peter and I talked for an hour. It was clear he was exhausted, confused and close to burnout. All his life Peter had worked hard and now disillusionment with work was hitting him hard. He described his symptoms as "feeling empty", "nothing to give", "massive self-criticism", "very tearful", "uninspired", "feeling stuck" and "no energy". Intuitively, I felt Peter was ready for a breakthrough.

"I am down on my knees," Peter said. Hearing these words gave me a really crazy idea. "Peter, let's pray," I said.

Imagine a psychiatrist and a psychotherapist praying on the

telephone! Together we gave God our life and our work, and we prayed for fresh inspiration, insight and guidance. It was a precious moment. Two days later, I received a thank-you note from Peter. The P.S. read: "God works in mysterious ways!"

There is a shift taking place in psychology today. Traditionally, the psychology profession has been suspicious of anything it cannot measure, analyze or define. God, being immeasurable, was kicked out of the laboratory for not being small enough. Psychology then tried to take the place of God without success. Today, a new generation of psychologists is open to exploring and reintegrating the spiritual in healing.

A similar shift is taking place in society too. Conversations about God are cool again. People are less afraid to explore God in an open, mature and non-dogmatic way. Spirituality is important to people. "Every day people are straying away from church and going back to God," said Lenny Bruce. This is true! But churches are also changing. A new generation of ministers wants less "churchianity" and more Christianity, less religiosity and more spirituality, less preaching and more direct experience.

I have often thought, what a pity it is we made a religion out of God. God is much bigger than religion. God cannot be bottled, labeled and sold. And yet religion has peddled some weird and fearful potions. And we bought them too! Thankfully, a shift is happening now. We are fast outgrowing our "small gods". We want the immeasurable God again.

I have discovered in my work that there is a level of your mind which is *all about God*—whether you are religious or not. I have found that whenever you clear your stuff about God, your life shifts. Life gets easier. To be happy you do not have to be religious about God, but you do have to be unafraid of God.

Fear is non-specific. Thus, for as long as you are afraid of God you will be afraid of everything. Projection of "God issues" can lead to other issues such as, 1) fights with authority figures like parents, the boss and the law, 2) denial of your own true authority and wisdom. At the deepest level, being at odds with God is also being at odds with yourself. Life is frightening. Death is frightening. And many illnesses and problems are really fears *raising a fist to God*.

To some, God is a fiction, a tyrant, an expletive, an aloof dictator, a heartless landlord, a cruel bully who fixes wars and football games. This is not God: this is ego. To others, *God is beyond ego*. God is immeasurable love, an infinite intelligence, unconditional peace, the creative impulse that supports the highest in everyone.

I would go so far as to say that if your God is not a God of love, get another God! What you want is a God that is bigger than your fear, your anger, your guilt, your ego, your self. When you play with a small god who is only as big as you are, God cannot fully be God to you. Let go, therefore, of your own ideas about God, and let *God teach you about God.*

When all else fails you try God, but maybe you should first try God before all else fails! God houses your immeasurable Self— your Unconditioned "you". When you reach to God, you are simply reaching to the highest in yourself.

Take ten minutes, now, to review a challenge in your life. Call to mind all your feelings, thoughts and fears. Now ask God, your highest Self, for some light. Imagine a light shining in your mind (a light with no "off" switch!) Relax, be wide open, and welcome a new idea, a fresh perception, a great thought, some humor, a more helpful perspective and a better way.

YOUR WORLD AWAITS YOU

Have you tried to change the world lately? How did you get on? Most people report some difficulty! This is especially true if you will not change first. After all, a mirror can only work with what you give it. Hence, the first law of personal alchemy states, *the world changes when you do.*

A mystic once wrote, "All your suffering is rooted in a single superstition which is that you believe you live in a world when in truth the world lives in you." Imagine for a moment that the world is not a physical place that is separate from you, that you enter in and out of, but, rather, the world is really a projection of your state of mind. If this is so, then your mind really can move mountains.

There are three dominant worldviews in psychology and philosophy. Each worldview is represented using the following formulas:

1. The world = my life = me
2. The world + me = my life
3. Me + the world = my life

The world = my life = me offers a bleak, limited view of who you are and what you are capable of. It smacks of determinism. It essentially states that the world happens and you respond as a conditioned reflex with no imagination, no choice, no adventure and no hope for a better future.

This worldview is Pavlovian. In his most famous experiment Ivan Pavlov, the Russian physiologist, rang a bell when giving food to dogs. The dogs' glands secreted saliva at the sight of the food. After some repetition, Pavlov's dogs salivated at the sound of the bell even though there was no food. This experiment led to the theory of conditioned response in humans. Apparently we humans are exactly the same as dogs, i.e., the world rings and we dribble.

In other words, the world determines how you shall be, and you have no say in the matter. Therefore, poor service at a restaurant *must* ruin your evening; an argument with your partner *must* mean you close down; bad traffic *must* cause road rage; two pounds' weight gain *must* cause an asthma attack; a hard week at work *must* ruin your weekend; public speaking *must* cause incontinence; fresh bird crap on your clean car *must* be a near-death experience; and a stain on your favorite dress *must* leave you inconsolable.

The world + me = my life is more hopeful. This worldview says the world happens, but you can choose to respond to what happens. Welcome to a world of choice!

This worldview recognizes that your thinking can make a difference. Now a parking fine is a nuisance and not a reason for atheism! Now a failed job interview is tough but not terminal! Now your football team losing is painful but not lethal! Now a fight with your partner leads not to war but to a declaration of love.

Cognitive psychology supports this second worldview. Cognitive psychology says your life is what your thoughts make it. In other words, *life is 10 per cent circumstance and 90 per cent response to circumstance.* This worldview is still limited though, because it defines you as an effect of the world (an effect with choice), when really you are the creator of the world. In truth, there is no world without you.

Me + the world = my life is the most exciting worldview of all. Here the world is defined as a mind-mirror. It is a projection of your own mind. The world is the hardware and you provide the software. You write the program and the world responds to you. You can be *micro-soft, micro-cool, micro-victim, micro-free, micro-love, micro-fear,* and the world will act accordingly.

This worldview says, *the world offers a perfect accommodation for all your thoughts*. Whatever you think, the world will mirror it. In particular, *you create the world in your own image*. For instance, if you think you are unlovable, the world will mirror this. If you think you are unworthy, the world will reflect this. If you think you must struggle, the world will accommodate this. *Change your thoughts, and you change the world.*

This worldview also supports the *domino effect*: 1) what you do to yourself, others will do to you too, i.e., people will treat you only as well as you treat yourself; 2) others will do to you what you are already doing to them. In this worldview the key is consciousness, not just action. This worldview also points out that if you are looking for the world to make you happy you will be disappointed. Why? Because the world is an effect, and you are the cause.

Today, decide to *be the difference* you are looking for. Think of something you would like to change. First, ask your higher Self, *"What is the real goal here?"* Be open to the bigger picture. Instead of waiting for change to happen, or insisting "they" change first, ask your higher mind, *"How can I be different here?"* Think about how you can show up differently so as to experience a difference.

THE MEANING OF LIFE IS MADE, NOT FOUND

I first met Freddie Frankl when the British Broadcasting Corporation (BBC) invited me to inherit his popular radio phone-in series on stress and well-being. My government-backed Stress Busters Clinic had been running very well for two years, and I was considered a suitable successor to Freddie who by then was in his early seventies and was finally retiring.

Freddie Frankl was a rare psychiatrist. For starters, he was happy! He was warm, kind, wholehearted and liked to laugh. He was famous for his motto, "One laugh is worth two tablets". Freddie was like a wise old owl. I learned a lot from him. I remember him on our last meeting before his death saying to me, "The search for *the meaning of life* is folly—the meaning of life is made, not found."

Freddie's uncle was the internationally renowned psychiatrist, Viktor Frankl, author of *Man's Search for Meaning* and founder of Logotherapy, heralded as "The Third Viennese School of Psychotherapy" after Freud and Adler. *Logos* is a Greek word which denotes "meaning". Viktor Frankl believed that man's search for meaning is the primary motivation in life.

Viktor Frankl was a survivor of the Nazi concentration camps. His horrific experiences taught him that people can survive any hardship if they are able to make a positive meaning out of it. "Even the worst circumstance can be transformed by our minds," he wrote.

The meaning of life is not a search—it is a choice. Meaning is not found in things; meaning is what you make of things. The world means nothing by itself. You give it all the meaning it has. Thus, the meaning of life is a choice you make, not just once, but every waking hour of your day.

Life is like art—it is all about interpretation. The moment anything happens to you, you interpret a meaning for it. The meaning you vote for then governs your perception, your thinking, your faith, your choices, your feelings, your behaviors, everything! Whenever you elect a new meaning, this changes everything. Here is a great key to healing and success.

An event occurs, and it is your interpretation and meaning that decide everything thereafter. "There is nothing either good or bad but thinking makes it so," wrote Shakespeare. For example:

- Two accidents in quick succession may mean God doesn't care, or, you need to take care.
- A boss who spends no time with you may mean he doesn't like you, or, he trusts you.
- When he/she doesn't call it may mean the romance is cooling, or, they are simply busy.
- A friend acting out of character may mean he/she doesn't love you, or, he/she is calling for help.
- Losing your lipstick might mean a world emergency, or, it's time to buy some more.
- A speeding ticket might mean the world is out to get you, or, you need to slow down.
- A stain on your shirt might mean a drama, or, nothing.
- A pink slip might mean the end of your life, or, a new beginning.
- Showing your emotions might be a sign of weakness, or, a show of strength.
- A failed job interview might mean you lost out, or, something even better is in store.

Your ego is an avid interpreter. It is so quick to interpret events as "bad" or "good", "wrong" or "right". It never fails to see "the little picture". This is particularly so during a "crisis" when so much judgment, fear, anxiety and panic blots your mind it is almost impossible to perceive your own best interests.

Whenever I experience any trouble, I try *The 180° Shift*. I look at what is troubling me, and I ask myself, *"What if "bad" is "good", "wrong" is "right," and this "trouble" is a "gift"?"* The fact is, *"This could mean anything."* Shifting my thoughts like this helps to suspend the ego's fear mongering. It also helps me to be open and receptive to higher thoughts.

Fear is not in things; fear is only in the meaning you give things. Pain is not in things; pain is only in the meaning you give things. Change the meaning, and the fear and the pain are transformed. Sometimes the greatest fear and pain come from a sense of meaninglessness in life. *Meaning is a choice, not a search*, remember? A sense of meaninglessness is really, therefore, a call to let in higher awareness and truth.

Right now, practice *The 180° Shift*. Think of a challenge, something "wrong", "bad", "painful" or "negative". Step one:

declare, "*This could mean anything.*" Step two: suspend all judgments and clear your mind. Step three: be open to higher inspiration, a new perception and a more positive interpretation. Doing *The 180° Shift* with another person can also be very beneficial.

WHAT YOU BELIEVE WILL BE
HOW YOU LIVE

Life is hard if you believe it has to be. Things are never easy if you insist. There are no free lunches if you say so. The struggle never ends if you want it that way. You are at liberty to believe whatever you want. This is called free-will. What you believe to be true is true *for you.*

You are a philosopher. And you have a philosophy about everything, including money, happiness, men, women, relationships, success, life, healing, sickness, business and love. You have had many teachers. You have learned much. You have also forgotten much. Your philosophy means a lot to you. It means so much to you that you probably wouldn't trade it for anything—*even happiness* !

Your most important philosophy is your philosophy about yourself. What you believe about yourself ultimately determines how your life must unfold. Your Self-belief governs what you think you deserve and don't; what is possible and isn't; what you attract and lose; what you are open to and miss. *What you believe will be.*

Each moment you are experiencing the effects of your beliefs. Nothing else is happening! Your beliefs are like magnets. They are affirmative. They attract what you think is right and true. Every belief is a self-fulfilling prophecy in life. I think of it this way: your beliefs are a film; your perception is the projector; and your life happens on the big screen.

An essential law of belief is, *what you believe will be what you perceive*. Belief and perception are like two best friends who collude about everything. Whatever belief says, perception confirms. In fact the function of perception is *to gather evidence to prove that beliefs are right*. Belief says to perception, "This is no good", and perception says, "You are so right!" Belief says, "This is very good", and perception says, "You are so right!"

If you believe life is hard, your perception will gather evidence to prove that, "You are so right!" If you insist that love hurts, your perception will tell you, "You are so right!" If you think there is no support, perception agrees, "You are so right!" If you say there are no available men, perception nods its head, "You are so right!" If you believe the world is your oyster, your perception smiles, "You are so right!"

Another essential law of belief is, *a belief has no power other than what you give it*. Without you a belief cannot exist.

Ultimately, you are in charge of your beliefs, but sometimes you give your beliefs so much credence and power that they appear to take on a life of their own. I call this *The Frankenstein Effect*.

Mary Shelley's *Frankenstein* is one of the best-known horror stories ever told. Dr. Frankenstein is a young scientist whose own life-giving creation becomes a savage monster that turns on him and the whole world. This story offers a good metaphor for the ego and its creations of fear. You create beliefs in the laboratory of your own mind, some of which are so limiting and so fearful they appear to turn on you.

To believe or not to believe, that is the question. Beliefs, perceptions and experiences will always collaborate so that you can be right about whatever you want. The point is, *do you want to be right or happy*? In other words, do you want to cling to old beliefs that cause pain and fear, or open up to new beliefs that are more joyous and liberating? The choice is yours.

Most people try to live in the present moment with a bag of beliefs that are at least twenty years out of date. Fortunately, *it takes only one loving thought to transform an entire belief system of fear.* A little willingness is a mighty power.

Shift happens when you change your beliefs. Your life changes. Everything changes. Pick a subject like "relationships", "happiness" or "success". First, make a list of every limiting, fearful belief you have about this subject. Also, see if you can pin an experience to each of these old beliefs. All fearful beliefs are old beliefs from the past.

Take each old belief that looks to be past its sell-by date, and ask yourself, "*Do I want to be right or happy?*" Now try this visualization. Close your eyes. Be very still. Take a deep breath. And picture a beautiful healing light shining into your mind and heart so there are no dark corners left. Imagine the screen of your mind is completely clear, and you can now insert another belief – another film. Now you can play a love story, a success story, or any story you like. Choose your belief, run the film, and live your life!

Your unconscious mind communicates predominantly with metaphor, dream and story. It enjoys these sorts of meditations and visualization much more than conscious logic. When you use imagination to clear your beliefs, your life can become even better than you can imagine!

THERE ARE NO EVENTS, ONLY PERCEPTIONS

I recently gave a one-day workshop in London called Quantum Leap. My own personal belief was that it was a great day if you are talking about the weather. My self-doubt and self-criticism were rabid all day. I believed I was uninspired—and my perception worked overtime to prove that my belief was right.

At the end of the day I was tired and sorry that I hadn't given my best. I was genuinely surprised, therefore, when the audience gave me such a generous ovation. I was even more surprised when several of my team told me it was my best workshop yet. Over the next three days, I received over fifty letters, faxes, emails and phone calls expressing gratitude. So my point is, *how could so many people get it so wrong?*

We all see things differently. Perception is highly subjective. In fact, there is no such thing as a single objective perception. Your point of view is a total one-off. In workshops I often illustrate how variable perception is with a perception test called "Count the Fs". Take a moment, now, to count how many Fs you see in the box.

67

COUNT THE Fs

FEATURE FILMS ARE THE RE-
SULT OF YEARS OF SCIENTI-
FIC STUDY COMBINED WITH
THE EXPERIENCE OF YEARS

The answer I am looking for is six Fs. Some say there are only three, four or five Fs, usually because they do not see the Fs in "of ", which appears three times. Those who think it is a trick question say seven Fs because they count six in the text and one in the heading. And then there was one person who counted twenty-seven Fs because he superimposed "F" on to "B", "R", "E" and "P"!

Your eyes are truly wondrous miracles of creation. The eye is operated by six delicate, strong muscles that perform over 100,000 movements a day to give you sight. Your iris, retina and optic nerves gather and organize information that is sent to your brain at over 155 miles per hour. Amazing as this is, your perception is not entirely physical. Indeed, perception is 99 percent mental.

The first law of perception is, *you see what you want to see.* Your eyes do the seeing, but it is your mind that decides what you focus on. In other words, *you see what your mind is looking for.* In effect, you never see the world; you see your thoughts! This realization alone is a great key to personal alchemy and success. Perception is projection.

The cynic and the optimist have never been able to agree on what they see. Both have a philosophy of life and both see things differently, but which one is right? The truth is, the cynic is right. The cynic sees exactly what he is looking for. He sees there is no hope in the world. The optimist is also right however! The optimist sees what he believes too. He sees a world of hope. *Both are right, and both are choosing their experience.*

There are no events, only perceptions. Fear is a perception. To the fearful eye, there is only danger. Love is a perception. Love sees truth, beauty and safety. Your childhood is a perception. Yesterday is a perception. Right now is a perception. Hope is a perception. Pain is a perception. Pain is also a signal to shift your perception.

There is always another way of seeing things. Your eyes blink twenty-five times a minute on average, so, you have twenty-five opportunities a minute to see things differently. Shift happens in the blink of an eye. And a really "big" problem can be overcome by a really "small" shift in perception. Whenever you are in pain, first choose peace, and then state, "*I am willing to see things differently.*" Be open.

What will you look for today? A beautiful exercise for each new day is to dedicate your perception to whatever it is you want most. For instance, if you want love, then pray for love to bless your perception. If you want peace, then ask your higher mind to guide you. If you want joy, then ask God to see for you. Whenever you change your mind, soften your focus and look through new eyes; you will see things in a new light.

CHOOSE THE HIGHEST THOUGHT!

Every day you make a thousand choices. You choose what to wear, where to go, who to meet, what to eat and what to do. Most important of all, you choose what to think. One thing is for sure, today will not be any better than your thoughts. Choose your thoughts wisely, therefore, *as you can only go as high as your thoughts.*

Look inside your mind and notice all the thoughts. It is estimated that your mind thinks at least 2,500 thoughts an hour all through your life. Unless you are in samadhi, deep sleep or a coma, your mind is thinking. Perhaps this is the problem. Maybe you are thinking too much!

Notice how your mind is full of thoughts of love, judgment, peace, fear, grace, guilt, joy, anger, forgiveness, attack, laughter, work, play, judgment, kindness, isolation, oneness, etc. In your mind is every thought in the world. Which thoughts are you identifying with right now? Which thoughts are you choosing to go with?

My work in psychology and healing has taught me that *mental health is the capacity to choose your thoughts.* The ability to choose your thoughts is the difference between pain and freedom. For instance:

- When your child crams another Oreo cookie into the video recorder, it doesn't ruin your day because you choose not to let it.
- A flat tire doesn't give you a headache because only you can give yourself a headache and you decide not to.
- A personal criticism could cause a cardiac arrest, but you choose to laugh it off instead.
- A computer crash could be the end of the world for ten minutes or a month. Your choice.
- A friend who lets you down could trigger Armageddon, but you choose otherwise.
- A bad hair day does not mean you have to write a suicide note because you know better.

In difficult times perception collapses and you lose sight of your choices. Fear plays tricks with the mind. Thoughts appear to take on a life of their own, running up one-way streets, getting lost in mental cul-de-sacs, hitting a wall and being beaten senseless in dead-end alleys. Your mind is out to get you. It is not a safe place. True perspective is shattered. There appears to be no choice.

When you are in trouble, *your thinking will never get you out alive.* What you need is faith. Faith is the willingness to look past your thoughts and see another possibility. Better still, it is the courage to stop your thinking altogether and let yourself be inspired and blessed and guided by something other than your ego, i.e., your higher mind.

Your ego uses a slow, limited form of thinking called *logic.* Logic is a device of the separated mind which believes that you have been left to think your life out all on your own. Your higher mind—the part of you that is unconditionally connected to all life—does not have to confine itself to singular logic. It is an Aladdin's lamp that uses inspiration, intuition, vision, eureka, miracles and love.

The greatest truth I have learned about happiness is that *happiness is only ever one thought away at most.* One fresh perception, one new belief, one innovative thought, one powerful decision, one moment of surrender, one instant of complete openness, is all it takes to experience a world of difference. Nothing but your thoughts can hurt you. Therefore, whenever you are in fear or pain you are being called to choose again.

Every day the world shows you your state of mind. Life comes right up to your face and says, "*This is what you are thinking—have a nice day!*" The good news is you are free to change your mind whenever you want. When you shift your thinking, the world shifts. This is because the world is an effect of your thoughts.

In every event, encounter or situation cultivate the habit of asking yourself "*What is the highest thought here?*" Be still an instant, lay aside everyday thoughts, delete the ego, release your fears, jettison your judgments and make yourself available to higher wisdom. Inspiration goes wherever it is made welcome.

KEEP SMILING—UNLESS YOU FEEL LIKE CRYING

I once met a woman who was suffering from "positive thinking". I was giving a talk called Choosing Happiness to a group of 500 nurses. Halfway through the talk, this woman stood up and screamed, "How do you expect me to be happy when my husband has died?" The room fell silent.

First I thanked the woman for having the courage to share her feelings. Then she told us her story. Her husband had died only three weeks before from an unexpected heart attack. Since his death she had "kept busy" by going on five different positive thinking courses. "Nothing works," she said. When I asked her if she had cried yet, she said, "No."

I invited the woman on to the stage, and together we looked at how she was using positive thinking to bully her feelings into submission instead of genuinely healing them. "I want you to give up positive thinking," I said. She looked absolutely dismayed. "What else can I do?" she asked. Before I could answer, she burst into tears. She cried so deeply, it was as if each teardrop carried away pieces of her grief and pain. There was barely a dry eye in the audience either.

Two weeks after the workshop I received a letter from the woman. It read: "Every day I experience the A–Z of pain, but I do what you say. I make time for my feelings now. I pray for help, my friends know how I really feel, and I am open to healing. Choosing happiness is about saying "yes" to my feelings—that way they heal faster." At the end of her letter she added a P.S. "Thanks for making me cry!"

At psychology school there was no time for emotions in our schedule. We had plenty of time for cognition, perception, memory, behavior and rats, but no emotions. Even rats were preferable to emotions! I have since learned that emotions are not just thoughts, and that "positive thinking" can often be misused in emotional healing. Emotions are mysterious, illogical and deep. They cannot just be thought away. They need to be accepted, loved and felt.

The first key to emotional healing is to *start where you are*. Your feelings are not getting in the way of your schedule; they *are* your schedule! What you are feeling is what you *should* be feeling. Sometimes healing takes precedence over your career, your social life, or any other plans you have. Give yourself space before your pain takes over your whole diary. Remember, on the other side of this pain is deep peace, greater abundance and more freedom.

The second key is, *be honest about how you feel.* One of the principles of my work at The Happiness Project is, *keep smiling—unless you feel like crying.* Another principle is, *you will never be truly happy if you are untruthful about your unhappiness.* And don't "logicalize" your feelings. For instance, to say "I am depressed" is not enough. Depression isn't a feeling. Be open to the feelings you are "depressing". With emotional healing, *honesty is the fast policy.*

The third key is, *feel your feelings all the way through to the other side.* A feeling only has one ambition in life, and that is it wants to be felt. Imagine telephoning a friend and being put on hold for five years. You would boil in your own stew. Well, imagine how your feelings feel when they are put on hold. *Feeling is the healing process.* To feel takes acceptance, openness and love, and, wherever they are, peace can eventually abide.

The fourth key is, *pain is resistance.* When you fight your feelings, it's you who always ends up hitting the canvas. What you refuse to feel will be expressed physically or unconsciously. What you try to avoid plagues you. Also, what you do not own for yourself you will project on to others, hence the saying, *hurt people hurt people.*

The fifth key is, *keep breathing because it improves your chances of happiness!* Mental "make wrong" and emotional resistance tend to create uncomfortable sensations in the body. The body feels what the mind feels, and the body blocks what the mind blocks. Let a deep, full breath be a symbol of your willingness to receive healing and let go of pain.

The sixth key is, *there is no such thing as a negative emotion.* Practice the golden rule with your feelings. In other words, treat your feelings the way you would like to be treated. Be kind, be courteous and be open to every feeling you meet. Feelings are like little people—*when you treat them well, they treat you much better.* They will also reveal gifts they might otherwise have withheld.

The seventh key is, *shift happens when you let go!* Feelings don't go; you let go of feelings. Whenever you are in pain, it is because you are clinging and holding on. Let your prayer be, "I am willing to let go now." Hand over all your thoughts, perceptions and beliefs to your peaceful Unconditioned Self, and affirm, "I am willing to be open to a beautiful lesson or gift here." Remember, you are not meant to heal alone. Healing is always about joining, connecting and choosing happiness.

BE THE GOAL!

The fastest way I know to prosperity, happiness and success is to commit to a principle I call "be the goal".

Despite daily practice, I am still not good at getting out of bed in the morning. When I travel, I need at least two wakeup calls. At home I have a CD alarm clock that wakes me up with something classical and loud! That said, my morning meditation is sacrosanct. It is the most precious time of my day. There is no busyness, no doing, no chasing, and no hurry. There is only stillness and *being*. It is in these moments I commit to *being the goal*.

Being the goal is about setting your intention for the day. It is about vision, clarity of purpose and *being what you want*. For instance, love is more important to me than anything. Therefore, each day I make it my intention to be a loving presence to everyone I meet. Every morning I pray that I may be a true friend to my friends, colleagues and family. Sometimes when I meditate I will ask, "Who needs my friendship today?" Other times a friend will pop into my mind, and I will pray "Dear God, show me how to be a true friend to — today."

Being the goal crystallizes the magnificent power of intention. It is the key to friendship, romance, leadership, success and everything. An eccentric friend of mine once said, "Robert, *do you want to be the sort of person who lights up a room when you walk in or when you walk out?*" That's what *being the goal* is about!

Laughter is important to me. I want to enjoy laughter, and so I commit to bringing happiness with me, i.e., *being happy*. Honesty, loyalty and trust mean a lot to me. To enjoy honesty, I understand I have *to be honest*. To have loyal friendships, I have *to be loyal*. To have trust, I have *to be trusting*. In other words, I aim *to be the goal*.

Today, be what you want.
If you want love, be loving.
If you want peace, be peaceful.
If you want fun, be funny.
If you want "new", be different.
If you want adventure, be open.
If you want success, be alive.
If you want joy, be kind.
Be what you want!

Life is all about *being first* after all! *Being first* is about consciousness, not competitiveness, i.e., "as you sow, so shall you reap". To be loved, you have to be willing to *love first*; to be cherished, you have to be willing to give *respect first*; to be heard you have to be willing to *listen first*; to experience forgiveness and freedom, you have to be willing to *forgive first*.

I honestly believe that *the only way to get to happiness is to be happy already*. Many people live their life according to the formula: Do + Have = Be. They cannot just *be happy* because first they must *do* "x" and *have* "y", i.e., "do a lot", "have a house", "do more", "do even more", "have a partner", "have lots of money", etc, etc. Why not just *be happy*?

With healing, people often convince themselves that they have to get well before they can choose happiness again. In my work I encourage my clients to honor pain *and* choose peace, feel fear *and* choose love, face the anger *and* choose forgiveness, experience the heartbreak *and* choose happiness, experience the guilt *and* choose innocence.

Ghandi once said, *"You have to be the change you want."* Why? Because the mirror cannot change without you. And the world is only a mirror. Remember, you see only your thoughts. *When you shift, shift happens.* It you don't, you simply experience more of the same. It is no good saying, "I'll be open with you, as soon as you are open with me." Be first. Be different if you want a different outcome. Be the goal.

What "to be" decisions will you make today? Think of your goals, your challenges, your relationships, and ask yourself, "*Is how I am being going to bring me what I really want?*" Be still a moment and reset your intention to be loving no matter what, to be kind in spite of everything, to shine your light come what may. Your "to be" decisions are between you and God. Let nothing steal them away.

GIVE UP YOUR FEAR OF GIVING

was at my health club on an exercise bike pedaling fast to nowhere when James first introduced himself to me. I will never forget that moment for as long as I live.

I was nearing the end of a grueling ninety minute workout. I was in a sweat, in a world of my own, and the last two minutes of the cycle program were feeling like forever. Sometimes I swear I can make time go backwards when I exercise! I had not noticed James and his companion enter the gym, so I was greatly surprised when James slapped me on the back and shouted, "Hellooo." It took all my balance just to stay on the bike!

James's hearty, open manner left me abashed. "Why pick on me?" I thought. As it turned out James didn't just pick on me. I watched him enthusiastically introduce himself to every person in the gym. "Hellooo," he said to the man who almost fell off the treadmill. "Hellooo," he said to the man who almost dropped his dumbbells. "Hellooo," he said to the most attractive woman in the gym whom no man dared to talk to.

James aimed his great big smile at everyone he met, and within moments he was talking to people I had never spoken to in months of visits. I was so impressed. James was so natural, so present and so open with everyone. "That's how I want to be," I thought. Come to think of it, I probably was like that once.

James is diagnosed with Down's Syndrome. According to society he is deficient and ill. He is certainly different, but I saw no trace of lack. That day in the gym he was more unconditional, loving and communicative than the rest of us "well people" put together. James gave himself fully and he got the best of us in return. He had no fear of giving.

I believe the purpose of life is to be like James. You are a gift-bearer, blessed with gifts of God, and you are here on earth to live fully and give fully—not just things, but *who you are. You are the gift.* My work has shown me over and over again that when people do not give themselves fully they experience lack, struggle, discontent, emptiness, isolation and illness. Do not sit on your gifts.

Your ego's greatest fear of giving is that *giving is losing.* Ego thinks, the more love you give, the less you have; the more joy you give, the more diminished you are; the more hope you give, the more you fade away; and the more support you give, the more it kills you. The ego clearly sees all giving as an amputation rather than an extension. However, this is not giving; this is *sacrifice*. It is sacrifice that leads to loss.

The truth is *giving is a treasure in itself*. For instance, when you offer your smile, it is your body that registers more "T" cells; when you give love, it is your heart that gets the message, and when you give praise to someone, it is your consciousness that is raised. *What you give to others you affirm for yourself*. Giving is receiving. There is no loss.

Another fear of giving is the idea that giving leads to rejection and hurt. This is true if you confuse giving with bargaining. When your giving has a price, you may gain or lose. And when you give to get, you may well be disappointed. For instance, if you give a favor unconditionally, all is well; but if you give it to get one back, expectations may be dashed. When you give unconditionally, it is impossible to lose.

Giving is your purpose. Think about it. If you arrive with nothing and you leave with nothing, then it makes absolutely no sense to waste all your powers in only getting. When life is only about getting, your heart muscle withers and you are seized with fear, disappointment and loss. Also, have you noticed that when you only try to get, you never feel as if you have enough. My philosophy is, *if you want to be poor, grasp; if you want to be rich, give.*

An essential law of abundance is, *only what you do not give can be lacking.* Has it ever occurred to you that what you are not getting—either from someone, something or somewhere—might be precisely what you are not giving? For example, your boss doesn't motivate you, but do you motivate your boss? Your partner doesn't compliment you, but do you compliment your partner? Your child never listens to you, but do you really listen to your child? Really?

When you stop giving, you lose. You are held back not by what you don't get, but by what you don't give. Giving is an affirmation. Giving is receiving.

Commit today to being more present and more open. Let what you give come through you rather than from you. There is no lack this way. Be truly unconditional in what you give so that there can be no fear or loss. Let your giving be your treasure. If you experience conflict, lack or struggle today, let go of expectations, demands and aiming to get something. Give yourself unconditionally. *You* are never diminished and *you* cannot lose.

THERE ARE NO SHORTAGES, ONLY A LACK OF WILLINGNESS TO RECEIVE

Are you a good receiver? Do you drink life in? Do you let people give to you? Can you let the good times roll? When it comes to letting life be really great, what's your threshold? What's your fear?

The following questionnaire is lighthearted and serious. Read it slowly, and notice if it presses any buttons.

How much happiness can you handle before . . .

- you start thinking, "*This is too good to be true.*"
- you start looking for holes in the road, i.e., you start waiting for the fall.
- you go out and buy a fan and some shit because you just know that . . .
- you question it all: "*Why am I this happy?*" and "Why is he being this nice? "
- you start to feel miserable because if you are happy it must mean you are about to be miserable again!

- you wonder, "*What have I done to deserve this?*" In other words, "Am I good enough for this?"
- you have to touch wood, take out more insurance and wear lucky charms.
- you start hearing your father say, "*Let's not get carried away.*"
- you start hearing your mother say, "*He's not the Messiah, he's a very naughty boy . . .*"
- you just know there will be tears before bedtime, i.e., this can't last.
- you start to feel so beautiful, so attractive, so gorgeous and so light-filled that it freaks you out.
- you almost feel guilty, but not quite!

I have not met anyone who finds it easier to receive than give. Genuine receiving is so much what modern society is not about. It *is* about surrender, being, stillness, total trust, an absence of striving, gratitude, living in the moment, innocence and wonder. Most people are just too busy to receive.

Receiving is the key to giving. If you do not receive, all your giving eventually deteriorates into sacrifice. And that's not all.

THERE ARE NO SHORTAGES,
ONLY A LACK OF WILLINGNESS TO RECEIVE

When you do not receive you feel isolated, there is no synchronicity, each day is a struggle, inspiration is lacking, life is stagnant, relationships cannot blossom, you attack people for not giving to you, God feels unreal, and you play the victim.

Receiving is all about letting go. To be a good receiver you have to be willing to let go of expectations, plans, demands, control, pride, unworthiness and addiction to struggle. Essentially put, you have to let go of your ego. *Your ego cannot have it all and survive!* This is because your ego is really a thought of lack. It is only your ego that stands between you and total abundance.

To receive, you must be willing to give up all thoughts of lack. Lack is the great illusion. In truth, *there are no shortages, only a lack of willingness to receive.* Lack is a projection of your own guilt (i.e., sense of lack). It is a mirage that fools your perception. When you let go of your ego, and surrender to your Unconditioned Self, all illusions of lack disappear. Nothing is missing, and you are worthy of everything.

True receiving recognizes that on a spiritual level, what you want is already there. There's no need, therefore, to hope for love, as love is already yours. Hope, instead, that you will surrender more deeply to love. There's no need to search for happiness, as happiness is already yours. Hope, rather, that you may accept happiness more fully. Also, do not hope for peace to come, as it is already yours. Hope, now, that you may simply let peace unfold. To receive is the most effortless act of all.

Today is a good day to give up all thoughts of lack. It is also a good day to give up your fear of receiving. Ask yourself, "*What do I want to receive more of?*" Take a moment to think of everyone who would benefit if you allowed yourself to receive more. What stops you from being a better receiver? What are you afraid of? Notice any fears, and be willing to let them go.

Surrender to receiving. Let life give to you, so you can give yourself more fully to life. Let your partner love you, so you can see who he or she really is. Let your friends enrich you, so they may grow too. Let your colleagues support you, so their talents can unfold. Let Heaven inspire you. And let God be God to you.

Receiving heals your ego, and it also inspires a whole new level of giving.

STOP IMPROVING YOUR LIFE— AND START LIVING!

*No amount of self-improvement can
make up for a lack of self-acceptance.*

Soon after my book *Happiness NOW!* was published, a jour-
nalist interviewed me on the subject of self-improvement.
She found what I said surprising and refreshing. Afterwards she
asked me to write 100 words on what she called my "unique
take" on self-improvement. Here is what I wrote:

> After living sixteen years, 5,844 days, on the
>   spiritual path;
> After sitting for 5,000 hours in earnest meditation;
> After reading 1,000 brilliant books on success,
>   happiness and love;
> After listening to 500 self-healing tapes;
> After attending 250 self-improvement workshops;
> After benefiting from 200 therapy sessions;
> After praying on my knees more than 100 times;

After going on twenty-five retreats;
After enduring ten fasts;
After suffering five colonic irrigations;
And after trying to forgive Mom and Dad more
    than once;
I finally got the key to happiness: RELAX!

Some people are so busy striving for self-improvement that they have no time for self-acceptance. They also have no time for laughter, happiness or even relationships.

Many times I have watched people use self-improvement as a covert form of self-attack—heavily laced with self-criticism, self-loathing and a denial of wholeness. Self-improvement often starts with a perception of lack (i.e., "I am not good enough", "I am not okay yet", etc.). Unless this perception of lack is changed, you always end up where you started from, *in lack*! No amount of self-improvement is enough. There is no rest.

I tell people who attend my seminars that my work is not about self-improvement; *it's about self-acceptance.* I honestly believe everyone is holy, everyone is blessed, and everyone is an angel. Self-acceptance feeds the inner garden of the soul. It clears away the debris of doubt, criticism, fear, judgment and ego.

With self-acceptance you live and grow spontaneously, naturally, abundantly.

Imagine if you were to practice unconditional self-acceptance! How would your life be? What's your fear? For most people the fear is "*all hell will be let loose*", i.e., without self-improvement "I'm not okay", "I'll slip", "I'll turn bad". Other common fears are that self-acceptance leads to complacency, arrogance, egotism, narcissism, "losing my drive", falling behind and not growing any more.

These fears are, in truth, smokescreens for a much bigger fear, which is, *with enough self-acceptance you will experience so much unconditional love it will blow your ego away*. Also, with enough self-acceptance you will experience uncontrollably high levels of creativity, orgasmic abundance and boundless bliss. Check it out!

Self-acceptance is your number one goal in life. Why? Because for as long as you believe there is something unacceptable about you, you will push away love, you will sabotage success, you will unconsciously conspire against joy, you will struggle, and you will never really find out who you are or what you are really capable of.

With self-acceptance, you fear you will lose something, but

really *you lose nothing and gain everything.* For instance, with self-acceptance, you lose your fear of lack, and gain wholeness; you lose judgment and guilt, and gain innocence; you lose your ego, and regain great creativity. With self-acceptance, you lose ground, and start to fly!

Self-acceptance transforms your perception of yourself. The more you commit to self-acceptance, the more you will begin to see that there is nothing about the real you that is wrong, bad, not okay or not enough. Self-acceptance inspires all sorts of personal alchemy and self-realization. *It is truly the most powerful act of healing, prosperity and love on the planet.*

Today, be willing to practice unconditional self-acceptance. Affirm "I am okay," even if you can't see it yet. Cease striving. Trust in your goodness. Relax into your wholeness. Above all, be kind to yourself. You do not have to do anything good, right or great to justify this kindness. Treat yourself the best you can so as to bring out the best in yourself. Shift happens with self-acceptance! Be kind to yourself.

DON'T SWEAT IT!

"I'm doing a lot of work on myself," said my client.

"Do you ever tire of working so hard on yourself?"
I asked.

"What do you mean?"

"Well, maybe all this hard work is somehow holding you back. Why not give up working so hard at self-improvement and see what a little self-acceptance does for you. In other words, GIVE YOURSELF A BREAK."

"You mean no more hard work," she said.

"Yes—only self-acceptance," I said.

"I'll work on it," she said.

The work ethic is a faith founded on an unholy trinity of blood, sweat and tears. In terms of consciousness, it is distinctly Neanderthal. Brute force is the answer to everything, including happiness. Creative problem solving is about extra muscle power. Success in anything is about extra effort.

Disciples of the work ethic believe in the labor of love, the school of hard knocks and power breakfasts. They think that happiness is an achievement, success comes from struggle, inspiration is perspiration, and abundance is born of pain and sacrifice. Apparently, nothing good can happen unless you "make it happen".

The work ethic is really like a cult. The ego is the leader. Devotees believe creation began with a big bang. Apparently everything is the product of a big bang. They also believe in a God who probably didn't rest on the seventh day. Work ethic slaves say that work is salvation. Apparently, work establishes worth. They abhor relaxation (called "downtime") because they say it is so unproductive.

According to the work ethic, effort is power. But what if too much "efforting" can actually block creativity, healing and joy? Maybe it is because you are so full of effort that there is no room for inspiration, new ideas, God, miracles, breakthroughs and a better way.

Has it ever occurred to you that you may be trying too hard? For instance, maybe you are trying too hard to heal something. Maybe you are trying too hard to be happy. Maybe you are trying too hard to be liked. Maybe you are trying too hard to succeed. Maybe you are trying too hard with a difficult relationship. Maybe you are trying too hard to lose weight. Maybe you are trying too hard to attract a partner.

Have you ever noticed that what you try hardest "to make happen" often gives you the most grief? Perhaps your excessive efforting betrays an inner conflict. For instance:

- You fear you don't deserve good things that happen easily, i.e., you must work for them.
- You feel unworthy about receiving, and so you try to earn things instead.
- Your dysfunctional independence stops you asking for help, so you simply work harder.
- You apply more effort because you are tired and cannot see smarter options.
- You are trying to control outcomes.
- You keep struggling because you are afraid of success and abundance.
- You are afraid to let go and surrender to something better.
- You lack trust in your innocence, the grand design, and in God's help.

With the work ethic, I really know what I am talking about. I remember the day a close friend of mine had the audacity to tell me, "Robert, you work as hard as your father drank." "That's projection," I said. I was so angry I knew my friend must be right.

My mother watched me as I tried to work myself into an early grave. Several times she sent me cards with the same message:

> *Consider the lilies of the field, how they grow; they toil not, neither do they spin: And yet I say unto you, That even Solomon in all his glory was not arrayed like one of these.*
> —MATTHEW 6:28-9

"Nice message," I thought, "but doesn't she realize that she has already sent me this?" The pattern of my life was "work, work, work, exhaustion . . . work, work, work, exhaustion . . . work, work, work, exhaustion." I was in a sweat and there was no space for inspiration, no chance for miracles, and no time for joy.

Today, let go of the belief that you need to work hard for everything. Swap effort for inspiration. Ease up on struggle. Focus on a relationship or goal you are trying too hard at. Give up trying to "make it happen" and make way for guidance and success. Commit to ease. Believe in effortless accomplishment. Make space for a better way and an easier way.

STRUGGLE IS A CHOICE

Stella won the prize for having experienced more struggle, set-backs and hard knocks than anyone else she knew. Her life was a drama, literally. Stella was thirty-something, single, four times engaged, a talented actress, out of work, a fast talker, very creative, suing her last business partner, not talking to her mother, a real whirlwind character, and struggling more than ever to "make my life work".

Stella had the face of an angel and the mentality of a combat soldier. Her life was like an army obstacle course. Romance was a minefield. Business ventures often bombed. Her health often troubled her. Lucky breaks quickly turned gangrenous. There was never any peace. And even the slightest good fortune or joy seemed to spark off a war somewhere in her life.

"All I want is happiness," Stella protested.

"If that is all you really wanted then you would have it," I challenged.

"Well, you don't think I choose all this struggle, do you?"

"Yes," I said.

"Well, maybe some people choose struggle but others have struggle thrust upon them," said Stella, trying her best to look innocent.

"Struggle is always a choice," I said. Stella argued I was wrong.

On about our tenth session together, Stella showed up angry, tearful and "very hurt". She had just had a fight with her best friend who had had the audacity to call her a drama queen. I took my life into my own hands and asked, "If what your friend said isn't true, why does it hurt so much?"

Stella countered, "Are you saying I am a drama queen?" Once again, she argued I was wrong.

Four days later, I received a registered parcel in the post. Inside was a tiara made of lightweight plastic, with gold glitter and fake jewels. The enclosed card read: "The drama queen wishes to abdicate her throne. Please help!" It was from Stella. She had finally declared peace. She was tired of struggle. She was ready to kick her habit.

"I think my problem is that if I don't have a problem I go looking for one," said Stella. Struggle is always a choice. *It is also a sign that you could be making a better choice.* Once Stella accepted that struggle is not just bad luck she began to transform her life. She looked honestly at old heartbreaks, old wounds, old beliefs—all the old stuff. She saw when, where and with whom she decided that life had to be a struggle. She was now ready to step into her true power.

Struggle is where the ego makes its home. Through struggle the individual "I" is defined; through drama the individual "I" makes a story; through suffering the individual "I" creates a philosophy; through pain the individual "I" tries to establish its worth; through endless fighting the individual "I" marks its territory; and, through continually making things harder than necessary the individual "I" is temporarily sustained. Of course in peacetime the ego vanishes.

Have you noticed how society tries to champion struggle? Do you ever catch yourself applauding the strugglers, and throwing rotten fruit and vegetables at those who enjoy abundance? Did you learn that struggle builds character, knocks you into shape, and rips the evil stuffing out of you, i.e., struggle is actually good for you? If so, no wonder you have felt too guilty and too unworthy to enjoy the fruits of life without struggle.

Struggle is resistance. Stella had confused struggle with commitment, struggle with willingness, and struggle with passion.

Everything she had struggled for she had secretly been resisting and pushing away. Struggle was her way of paying for what she feared she didn't freely deserve. Ultimately, she used struggle as a defense against having life too good (and feeling too guilty!).

For as long as you struggle, you cannot claim your true power. Struggle is unnatural to the Unconditioned Self. It is unnecessary and never justified. Struggle is all about the "little picture", the "mini me" and the ego. Struggle is all about separation. With struggle, there is no joining, no synchronicity, no blessedness, no divine inspiration, no transcendence and no creative synergy! You never get to travel at the speed of light.

Struggle is a sure sign that you are in sacrifice. *It is also a sign that there is a better way.* Shift happens when you give up struggle. Put this book down in a moment, and give your relationship to struggle to God. Affirm, "*Just for today I will not struggle. Every time I am tempted to struggle, I will smile. And then I will choose peace.*" Struggle is a choice, and so is peace.

MARTYRDOM ALWAYS ENDS IN TEARS

Martyrdom always looks so handsome and noble from a distance, but close up it is ugly. If you have ever lived with a martyr, or tried to be one yourself, you know how ugly and painful it can get. With martyrdom, no one really wins. Everyone loses. Sacrifice is all about loss, and it always ends in tears.

Sacrifice is not a viable solution. It never really works. Any success is temporary. You can manipulate a situation for a while using sacrifice, but ultimately the cost is too high for everyone concerned.

In my work I have seen people try to use sacrifice to save a marriage. It appeared to work at first, but love and lies are not good bedfellows. I have seen children get ill in an attempt to heal their parents' relationship. I have seen lovers try to play small in a relationship so as to heal power struggles and avoid rejection. I have counseled great business leaders who almost died for their company. And I have also worked with people who tried to sacrifice their heart for success.

There can be no happy endings when you use sacrifice to win happiness, love and success. Think about it: *how can sacrifice be the key to wholeness?* Sacrifice is simply a mistake—a poor strategy that ends in lack and loss. The key to genuine happiness, love and success is to give up sacrifice.

Every time you are tempted to play the martyr, read the following ten thoughts about sacrifice. Hopefully you will change your mind.

1. *Sacrifice is of the ego.* The ego is your limited self-concept. It is a thought of separation and lack. Sacrifice is a "little idea"—and it is evidence that you are not thinking with your whole mind.

2. *There is no need for sacrifice.* The role of martyr is always self-appointed. Sacrifice is never really justified because *there is always a better way.*

3. *Sacrifice means everyone loses.* If you lose, then everyone loses. In truth, there is no such thing as a lose/win in relationships. The only reason not to believe this is if you still believe you are separate from everyone.

4. *Sacrifice is not love.* It looks like love, but it can't be because when you are in sacrifice or playing small or deliberately losing, you are not giving yourself. When you give yourself fully, without conditions, you don't lose.

5. *Sacrifice is fear.* Where you are in sacrifice is where you are afraid. What are you afraid of ? Maybe fear of rejection, fear of failure, fear of loss, or maybe, fear of happiness, fear of success, fear of playing big.

6. *Sacrifice is guilt.* Sacrifice is a way of trying to pay for what you think you don't deserve. It's a way of trying to make sure that success, happiness and love don't spoil you. Unfortunately, if you believe this, no amount of sacrifice is ever enough.

7. *Sacrifice is not giving.* Sacrifice is not a gift; it's a trade. When you play the martyr, your giving becomes more and more conditional, full of hidden emotional invoices that must be returned within twenty-eight days, hours, minutes, seconds . . .

8. *Sacrifice is control.* Sounds strange, but maybe you are using sacrifice as a way of controlling relationships, avoiding intimacy, staying separate, holding on to the past, and not letting go. Maybe sacrifice is a fear of uncontrollable bliss!

9. *Sacrifice always ends in loss.* People in sacrifice always end up demanding that everyone else sacrifice too. They will swear they don't, but it's true!

10. *Sacrifice is not your gift.* When you believe in martyrdom, giving feels like losing, commitment feels like chains, love feels like duty, and nothing is heartfelt. Your gift is to love, not lose.

Shift happens when you drop sacrifice. Ask yourself,

"Where am I in sacrifice at present?" What are you trying to get? Admit your sacrifice is not working. Give up your sacrifice to God, and be open to a better way. Imagine the whole universe supports you in shining, receiving and living life fully. Every time one person gives up sacrifice, we all win.

THERE ARE NO PROBLEMS, ONLY OPPORTUNITIES

I first met Mr. Chow in Switzerland at an international business conference where we were both speaking. Mr. Chow bears a striking resemblance to Hotei, the Laughing Buddha. He is of medium height, very plump, very jolly, and he wears a most marvelous radiant smile on his very round face. When he laughs his whole body dances and shakes.

Mr. Chow is a gifted Asian businessman. When he talks you want to listen. For two hours he regaled his audience with a most enchanting talk on "Creative Problem-solving". He told us, "Where I come from we use the same word for both "problem" and "opportunity". We teach our children that *there are no problems* because every problem is really a secret opportunity which encourages you to grow, prosper and be free."

There were two other things Mr. Chow said about creative problem-solving that were of real interest to me. The first was, "*Problems only happen to those who believe in them*"; and the second was "*There is no problem you don't really want, and there is no problem you can't really solve.*" I found what he had to say both challenging and helpful.

Do you believe in problems? Have you been conditioned to think that problems are necessary, unavoidable and a natural part of life? Can you even conceive of a life with no problems? Problems are society's number one employer. Society is full of troubleshooters, consultants, specialists, experts, diplomats and counselors. Imagine no problems!

My psychology training was all about problems. We played "spot the problem" with everyone. Anyone without a problem was dismissed as being in denial, repressed or dead. We were cautioned to believe that everything is a potential problem. I remember once reading a psychology paper on the dangers of laughter. Apparently excessive laughing may, in certain conditions, cause high blood pressure. A psychologist without a problem is like a dog without a bone.

Problems are not natural. They are evidence of internal conflict. My work has taught me that *any problem is on one level a form of self-attack*. Problems give life to your negative thoughts; they compound your belief in struggle; they confirm unworthiness; and they incite yet more fear. It is possible, however, to give your problems a higher purpose. As Mr. Chow says, you can use problems as opportunities "to grow, prosper, and be free".

The moment you make anything into a "problem", you define yourself as a victim. Notice how your perception is full of fear, doubt and anxiety. Consciously and unconsciously you are working overtime to look for pain, pitfalls and unhappy endings. On the other hand, the moment you make anything into an "opportunity" you open yourself up again to inspiration, gifts, lessons, new options and a way out.

There are no problems, only opportunities. This is what a true alchemist believes. One of my favorite authors, Ernest Hemingway, advised writers to use every joy, every pain and every experience as an aid to write better. Similarly, it is possible to use everything that happens to you as an opportunity to live better. The key is to stay open for long enough.

Think of a current "problem". Call it an opportunity. Be open for a possible gift. Perhaps it is really an opportunity to communicate better, ask for help or try something new. Or maybe it is an opportunity to be honest, authentic and more open. Or maybe it is an opportunity for surrender, prayer, healing, miracles and genuine soul guidance.

Be open for a better way. Be willing to look at it differently. Sometimes a really "big" problem can be overcome with a really "small" shift in perception. Be willing also to go for a higher thought. It was Einstein who said, "No problem is solved at the same level it was created at."

From now on, train your mind to believe that *there are no problems, only opportunities.*

FEAR IS YESTERDAY

In 1989 I opened the first Stress Busters Clinic, paid for by the National Health Service, in Great Britain. Over the next few years I worked closely with people who suffered from stress, anxiety, depression, heart disease, cancer and AIDS. The clinic quickly gained an excellent reputation. We won government sponsorship; the BBC broadcast a thirty-minute *Stress Busters* TV documentary; and my book *Stress Busters* became a best-seller.

If I could sum up what I learned, it would be: *fear is the root of every illness, every pain and every problem.* Look behind every stress, angst and anxiety and you will find fear lurking there. At a certain level, there are no problems, only fear; there are no illnesses, only fear; there are no conflicts, only fear; and, there is no devil, only fear. Heal the fear, and you rediscover your freedom.

Fear is frightening! Even more so if you refuse to look at it. Fear plays tricks on your mind. Perception is easily fooled by fear as it conjures up a hell, magics away all hope, and makes illusions of powerlessness. Fear will dress you up as a victim of the world. Yet you are not a victim of the world; you are the light of the world. Your light cannot be diminished by any amount of fear.

The most important thing to understand about fear is, *fear is yesterday*. When you are totally present, the mind is perfectly clear and whole. There is no split, no fear, no doubt and no angst. When you are afraid, it is because you are not present. Fear is always referencing the past. Fear is always counseling you against the perils of "now" because of something that happened once "before".

> *Fear is yesterday.* For example, I have counseled women who were afraid to start dating again, not because they couldn't find anyone but because their last relationship was so painful.

> *Fear is yesterday.* I have counseled men who were afraid to commit to marriage, not because there was no love, but because their parents had divorced and they were afraid of the same fate.

Fear is yesterday. I have counseled people who gave up carpe diem for cynicism and defensiveness because of unresolved hurt. Defenses always hide old wounds and old fears.

Fear is yesterday. I have counseled financially well-off people who habitually overwork, not because they need to but because they once had no work, or because they grew up poor.

Fear is yesterday. I have counseled people who were afraid to start anything new, not because they had no talent but because of past failures and recriminations.

Fear is yesterday. I have counseled people who were afraid to be happy now, because the last time it all ended in tears.

Fear is yesterday. I have counseled people who resisted feeling well again for fear of more pain, more heartbreak and more illness in the future.

Fear is yesterday. I have counseled people who do not follow their dreams because of old self-doubts, old self-criticisms, old beliefs and old fears.

According to the fear lobby (the one inside your head), fear is necessary, fear is good, and fear will keep you safe. In fact, fear is your one and only obstacle to joy. When you give up the belief that fear is necessary, you are letting go of the inner oppression that causes all pain. Healing is release from fear.

Fear is an inside job. It is a form of "small thinking"—an *ego virus* that blocks inspiration, impairs vision and causes countless errors of judgment. It betrays an allegiance with ego and not your Unconditioned Self. *Fear is not in things; fear is in the meaning you give things.* Hence, fear vanishes when you ask your higher mind to reinterpret all your perceptions, thoughts and meanings for you.

Be present; be powerful. Face your fears and let go of yesterday. Whenever you are in fear, ask yourself, "*Is this fear a fact, or is it just a fear?*" Remember this—a fear is often a *fantasy experienced as real.* First, feel the fear. Second, say, "Thank you for sharing!" Third, open yourself up to inspiration, soul guidance, a higher thought and God's help. Fear is always a call for help.

THE WORLD HAS FINISHED WITH YOUR PAST...IF YOU HAVE

I once had the pleasure of meeting the personal physician to His Holiness the Dalai Lama. We spent a whole afternoon together sharing insights and experiences from our life and work. At one point I asked him what he considered to be the key to health and happiness. He replied, *"Empty your bowl of yesterday's rice."*

What is yesterday's rice? It is your past. In particular, it is all your old disappointments, grievances and wounds. Every day at work I counsel people who are haunted by the ghosts of the past. Their mind is full of sticky rice. They hold their past against themselves, cruelly replaying mistakes, failures, heartbreaks, errors and moments of weakness.

There is an old saying, *all pain is old pain; all fear is old fear.* Whenever you are unhappy, you are probably replaying old movies in your mind. If when you are in fear or pain, you can have the presence to say, *"This is about the past,"* you immediately create an opening in your mind for healing, inspiration, forgiveness and something new.

Healing is a release from fear. It is also a release from the past. In truth, the past is over. It has been and gone. It is true to say, *the past is literally "all in the mind"*. Unless the past is over in your mind, however, you will be stuck on re-runs and you will miss new possibilities, new gifts and new adventures. Now is always a good time to forgive, to let go and say "yes" to life again.

Every time you let go of the past you step into greater freedom and greater creativity. You enjoy more energy. You feel alive again. You reconnect to the Unconditioned You. You are available now for new gifts. You attract more opportunities. And you are ready to experience a future unlike your past. *Shift happens—when you let go.*

Forgiveness releases you from the past. When you meditate on forgiveness, you learn that, in fact, *there is no past in the MIND of God.* In other words, your past is never held against you *unless you make it so.* Guilt is a choice; and so is forgiveness. When you choose guilt, you bury your gifts, live in fear, and everyone misses what you could offer. When you choose forgiveness, everyone can win again.

How do you know if you are holding on to your past? You are unhappy! When you are struggling, ask yourself, "*What am*

I holding on to from the past?" What old thought, old block or old fear are you still clinging to?

Another good "ghost buster" is this exercise. When you feel fear, let the fear speak to you as you repeat the following sentence: *"I am afraid of ___ because in the past I ___?"* Keep saying the sentence over and over and watch the old fears appear. Each time a fear appears, simply acknowledge it and be willing to let it go.

When you are cynical and defensive, repeat the following sentence: *"I have given up on ___ because in the past ___?"* When depressed, repeat: *"I am depressed now because in the past ——"* Once again, the idea is to make conscious your buried past so that you can erase, forgive and let go of old stuff. True forgiveness is a great *ghost buster.*

Unless you let go of your past, there will be no mystery about your future. Your life will be like the movie *Groundhog Day* where every day is just like yesterday. The members of your cast may change from time to time, but your story will essentially remain the same. Shift happens when you affirm "The Past is Over!" and "Now is New!"

People who come to my public seminars often hear me say, *"The world has finished with your past, if you have."* The moment you let go of your past, you stop projecting it on to the present. Now, as if by magic, a whole new world opens up for you. True healing, true forgiveness and true freedom are all about seeing that the past is not here any more. Now really is a new beginning.

To let go of your past, do these three things. First, be willing to forgive yourself for every mistake you think you ever made. Affirm "The past is over" and let forgiveness wipe away all tears. Second, if you want to be free of your past mistakes, free everyone from theirs. In other words, forgive everyone. Third, pray, "Dear God, I'm back!" Now let yourself be innocent again, free again and ready again to say "yes" to new healing, new happiness and a new future.

HEAL IT WITH YOUR FAMILY!

Whenever you heal any relationship, your whole life improves—and that counts for double with family.

Every year, for the past twelve years, I have vacationed on the tropical garden island of Kauai, in Hawaii. I stay with my friends Tom and Linda Carpenter. They are like family to me. On my first ever visit they urged me to try a legendary Hawaiian *Lomi Lomi* massage—a four-hour extravaganza of bodywork, meditation, prayer and other sacred rituals. It was pure bliss. In particular, it transformed the way I think about family.

Alan, a Kahuna priest, came highly recommended. To get to his home you have to drive through jungle, over bridges and alongside a river until you come to a clearing. Alan is a big man—big body, big smile, big heart, big hands, big spirit—big! He also gives you a big welcome. His whole family is there to greet you. "Before we work together, I want you to meet my family," he says.

"The body is like a family," Alan said as he massaged my spine. "Everything is family. Heart and lungs are family. Body and mind are family. You and me are family." Alan's words massaged my mind while his hands massaged my body. "Relax, Robert," he said, "let go of your grievances and make the body light again." Over and over Alan would massage and pray, massage and pray. "We are all family," he would say.

During the *Lomi Lomi*, Alan shared with me a sacred family ritual of the Hawaiian people. "At night, before sleep," he said, "the whole family sits in a circle. First, we share our gratitude and appreciation for the day. We celebrate the gifts we have received and given. We say "Thank you" to each other. And we say "Thank you" to God."

"Next," said Alan, "we share any sadness or pain from the day. The family joins in letting any grievance go. We say "I am sorry" to each other. We forgive, we let go." As Alan talked, I thought how wonderful it would be if doctors gave this family ritual out on prescription. Imagine a daily dose of gratitude and forgiveness. Imagine how well you would feel.

"Everything connects to everything," said Alan. I believe him. For instance, there is a strong connection between the breakdown of the family and our terrible mental health epidemic. "Family lives in your heart," said Alan. Yesterday's grievances, the unhealed anger, the unexpressed love and gratitude that rip a family apart also rip apart the individual family members. "There is no separation," said Alan.

After the *Lomi Lomi*, I drank tea with Alan and his family. I noticed how his children showed such natural, loving respect for Alan and his wife. By contrast, I remembered how as a child I was in constant judgment of my parents. Every day they did something "unfair", "wrong", "old-fashioned" or "embarrassing". All my friends were busy doing the same. Isn't it amazing how teenagers, in particular, know how to live better than their parents!

Family is where everything happens first: laughter and tears, happiness and heartbreak, gratitude and grudges, joining and competition, forgiveness and revenge, love and judgment. Family is the practice ground for making peace with yourself, and with the rest of the world. Most of us do not have rituals like Alan and his family. Hence, we do not grow out of judging and fighting with our family until after childhood, or maybe never.

Unless you heal it with your family, you will project your unfinished business on to everything that is current in your life—relationships, career, health, finance, everything. If this principle does not appeal to you, then it is for you! The truth is, you never really grow up until you make peace with your family. Bottom line is, you can't carry grievances and find peace; you can't attack and love; and *you can't be a victim and be happy*.

It is never too late to make peace with your family—even dead family members. A family is not just for life; it is forever. Remember, your family lives in your heart, i.e., your family goes wherever you go. Thus, the greatest gift you can give yourself is to forgive and let go of all family grievances. It is a true test of maturity to say, "*Love means more to me than any grievance I have about you.*"

Tonight, be willing to thank and forgive your family for everything. First, search deep for all the gifts your family has given you. Honor each family member. *Receive their gifts.* Next, be willing to forgive and let go of all family grievances. Let go now. Give away pain for love. Give away conflict for freedom. Give away anger for peace. Give away the old for something new, something better. It's your move. It's your choice.

YOUR GRIEVANCES HOLD
YOU BACK

Grievances often seem justified at the time but ultimately they cost too much, they are not worth the upkeep, and they cannot give you what you really want.

I have counseled people who have experienced terrible abuse, rape, torture, abandonment, betrayal and all sorts of injustice, and still I would say that *no grievance is worth holding onto*. No grievance, however justified, is worth the pain, hate and fear you must carry with it. Grievances cost too much. They are not worth giving up your freedom for.

A grievance is when your ego hijacks your mind, takes you to hell, demands a ransom, and leaves you there anyway. There you are, kidnapped by your own ego, sitting in hell hoping the "bitch" or "bastard" who is the cause of the grievance ends up in hell too. The great hope is you can both live *unhappily ever after*. Revenge is not victory; it is not freedom; it is not clever.

Every grievance is an attack on yourself. Carrying a grievance is like carrying a grenade that blows up every few seconds in your own mind. You are armed and dangerous, cloaked in hate, your own worst enemy. Why? *Thoughts do not leave their source.* All your bombs of anger, resentment and hate "go off" in your own mind, *hurting you first* before anyone else. Your enemy is hit only by residual debris.

For as long as you carry a grievance you become a casualty in your own war. Cells, nerves, heart, peace of mind and vision are always injured by the "friendly fire" of your own grievances. And yet, some people would rather die than give up a grievance. When asked, "Would you rather be right about your grievance, or happy?" they say, "I am right!" Their ultimate victory is not happiness, but, rather a tombstone bearing the epitaph, "I was right!"

For as long as you decide to carry a grievance you are wrong about yourself. A grievance is a sign of mistaken identity. If you hold on to a grievance, it must be because you think you are a victim. As long as you want to believe you are a victim, you will attract more wars, more enemies, more victimizers so as to prove your point. However, *you are not a victim, you are free.* This is what forgiveness teaches you.

Grievances hold you back. They muddy the mind with so much hate and fear that you begin to lose sight of your true purpose. Grievances are like mental cataracts. They distort your vision. You lose your focus. You look for revenge, not freedom; guilt, not innocence; hate, not wisdom; fear, not love. You are no longer held back by the love you didn't get, but by the love you are now not giving.

Holding on to any grievance is really a decision to suffer. Grievances will poison you as carrier, chain you to your past, and leave your perception bitter and twisted. Every day of your life you choose between grievances and freedom, pain and joy, the old and the new. Ask yourself, therefore, *"What do I really want?"* What will you make real? The willingness to let go of a grievance sets miracles in motion.

The first step towards going beyond grievances is to realize that a grievance is not a solution. It offers nothing of value to you. Forgiveness is the perfect antidote to any grievance. Forgiveness is the choice for wholeness. Forgiveness helps you affirm, 1) "I am whole"; 2) "No one and nothing can threaten or damage my wholeness"; 3) "My freedom is more important than any revenge." Forgiveness releases the pain of the past and wins you back your freedom.

Take a moment now to think of someone with whom you are annoyed, upset, angry or disappointed. Without any self-judgment whatsoever, let yourself feel the full extent of your grievance. Be honest about your feelings and notice how much this grievance hurts you both. Notice how split your mind is: a part of you wants to hold on to the grievance and a part of you wants to let it go. Experiment now with letting the grievance go.

In your mind's eye, picture this person standing before you. Imagine you are both surrounded by a beautiful, soft, healing light. Let this light be a symbol of unconditional peace. Imagine that what you both really want is peace. Look into each other's eyes, past the grievances, to the place where you are one with each other. Now affirm, "Together we choose peace instead of pain." Feel this with every cell of your being.

Your whole life shifts whenever you give up a grievance. In truth, every grievance is a temptation to stray from wholeness to lack, love to fear. It is a sign of inner conflict. Thus, whenever you are tempted to make an enemy out of anyone, it is good to affirm, "*I will not use you to hold me back.*" This way you really do choose peace instead of pain.

FORGIVENESS GIVES YOU WINGS

Forgiveness is a miracle worker that can literally change your life. Mind you, forgiveness is not for everyone. It is only for those who would like to experience total peace, creativity, love, bliss, healing, freedom and so on.

One of my most beautiful experiences of forgiveness happened to me in Finland while I was on a workshop tour organized by my friend Marika Burton and the magazine *Voi Hyvin*. It was early evening. I was alone in my hotel room. Marika had just phoned to say she could not come to dinner. My evening was now free. I decided to meditate for fifteen minutes before ordering some food.

I settled into a comfortable chair, closed my eyes, became still, inhaled deeply, and immediately I became aware of a thought: "*What would it be like to experience total peace?*" Two more thoughts quickly followed: "*Forgiveness heals all grievances*" and "*Forgiveness gives you wings.*" I felt in a good space, life was great, I had no big troubles, so I thought, "*Well, I've got fifteen minutes, so why not let go of all my grievances and see what happens?"*

Four hours later I still had not finished! One by one, every old grievance, complaint, gripe, niggle, judgment and humbug appeared spontaneously before me. For four hours I watched a special documentary of all my worst moments. Everyone was included! All my friends, every possible family member going back three generations, an old history teacher, an ex-boss, inept sports officials, unscrupulous salesmen, builders who charged too much, countless politicians, tax officials, airport staff, difficult clients, etc.

First, each person would spontaneously come to mind. I then witnessed a replay of the old grievance. Afterwards I affirmed, "I choose peace instead of this." As I did this, I felt a wave of forgiveness flow over us both. Every in-breath became a symbol of my willingness to accept forgiveness, healing and peace; and every out-breath became a symbol of my willingness to let go of old pain, old fear, old stuff.

By the time I had finished, I was sitting on top of bliss mountain. I had so much energy coursing through my body I could have sung an opera. My mind was totally free of judgment, fear, doubt and pain. My heart was expanding beyond the edges of my body. I felt so much peace it was as though I had no body. I was so happy I could have disappeared.

Forgiveness is a way of seeing. It offers an uncommon perception of yourself and the world about you. It goes beyond appearances to a greater truth. Forgiveness shows you that nothing can hurt you save your own thoughts, and forgiveness can shift all thoughts. Forgiveness reveals your original wholeness—a wholeness that cannot be damaged or hurt by anything in this world.

Forgiveness takes you beyond your own ego. Forgiveness offers insurance against bitterness, resentment, premature ageing, cynical rot, heart disease, an unhealed past and an unhappy future. It cancels excess baggage. It gives you wings. And it also offers you protection against an unforgiving mind that uses anger for energy, fear to navigate and pain to judge everything by.

Forgiveness is the switch. Forgiveness can switch you from ego to Unconditioned Self. It can switch fear to love, pain to peace, past to present, despair to freedom. Press for "forgiveness" and shift happens. Forgiveness is like a reset button that transforms your perception and gives you back your freedom, your sanity and your power. With forgiveness, you win.

Whenever I am asked, "How do you forgive?", I reply, "You don't." Forgiveness is not a technique. It is not something *you* make happen. Forgiveness requires no expertise, only willingness. It requires no effort, only intention. Forgiveness is an intelligent archetype. It knows what to do. All you have to do is make way for forgiveness. In other words, forgiveness forgives for you.

Forgiveness is victory. It is wisdom in action. It helps you to fly. It gives you gifts no amount of grievance can do. Above all, remember, "*Whenever I forgive anyone—it sets me free.*"

COMMIT TO LIVING
"HAPPILY EVEN AFTER"

For four years I ran an in-house counseling practice for the BBC. One of my clients was a TV producer called Claire. When I first met Claire, she was still in shock. In the space of six months, she had had a miscarriage, her husband had left her, both her parents had died, and her best friend was killed in a car crash. Claire had shut down. "It's all too much," she said.

Claire was clearly in emotional overwhelm. Her only coping strategy had been to get busy with work. She used busyness as "behavioral valium" to shut off her feelings. In effect, Claire had hung a "Closed" sign over her heart. She had closed the door on her feelings, herself, her husband, men, love, everything except work. Eventually, her work began to suffer too. She had unwittingly closed the door on her creativity, inspiration and flair.

Claire had reached a fork in the road. Either she could close down completely now and become one of the living dead, or she could dare to open up, heal and start over. She had to choose whether to live or die.

"If I let myself cry, I might never stop," said Claire. After shock comes grief. Claire cried constantly for a whole month. She wore minimal makeup. Her friends said it suited her. Next, after the grief came anger. "Why me, Robert?" she screamed. I supported Claire in letting go of her shame around her anger and her tears. Shame is the greatest obstacle to healing and full recovery.

"What did I do to deserve all this shit?" Claire asked. Deeper issues of guilt and self-doubt followed after anger. "Am I being punished?" "Am I really that bad?" I assured Claire that *bad experiences do not mean you are a bad person.* "What does it all mean, then?" Claire asked. "This is for you to decide." I told her. In particular, Claire had to decide whether or not to believe again in herself and in happiness.

"What I want is a sign!" said Claire. "I'll say "Yes" to life again if life gives me a sign."

"Like what?" I asked.

"How about a small win on the lottery?" she laughed.

In our next session, I asked Claire if she had won the lottery. "Well, I didn't enter," she said sheepishly. I told Claire I admired her unusual optimism. I also suggested that life would give her a sign if she first gave life a sign, i.e., like buying a ticket!

A month later, Claire arrived for her session with a big smile on her face. She showed me her lottery ticket. She had even bought one for me too. Claire had successfully navigated through four common stages of living *happily even after*: 1) shock and shutdown; 2) grief and sadness; 3) anger and attack; 4) guilt and self-doubt. Many times Claire had been sorely tempted to close the door, but to her credit she stayed open. Now she was ready for the final stage.

Claire's last obstacle to living *happily even after* was her resistance to joy. Could she trust in joy again? Could she trust in her own innocence and worthiness again? I have learned in my work that every pain, problem and trauma involves some resistance to joy. Claire had to open wholeheartedly to joy again, good times again, love again. She had to choose life.

"Shit happens!" says the car bumper sticker. Yes, it does. In fact, if you have made it to thirty, the chances are you already have enough reasons to be miserable to last a lifetime. And if you have made it to fifty, you probably already have enough reasons to be miserable for the next lifetime too! You have to ask yourself, "*What will I do with these reasons?* " Will you cash them in or will you let them go? Will you live *happily even after*?

Some life events, like divorce, bereavement, redundancy, a prison sentence, ill health, are enough to tempt anyone to close the door on life. No one ever told you that pain could hurt this much. And yet, if you close the door you lock yourself in and you suffocate on the old pain. Closing the door protects you from nothing. Eventually, you have to make a better choice.

When you commit to *happily even after,* you are really choosing happiness over history. You are leaving the past exactly where it is—in the past. You are also declaring: "I will not use the past to define who I am, what I deserve, or what is possible now." Now is new. What will you do with it? Will you close *down* or will you open *up*?

Scan your life intuitively for times when you have closed the door on success, happiness and living life fully. Look in particular for times when you experienced pain, failure, loss or rejection. Feel how tempted you were to shut down, play safe and shrink. Feel the feelings all the way through to the other side and then flip the "Closed" sign over to "Open".

SHIFT HAPPENS—
WHEN YOU LET GO!

At my Stress Busters Clinic, I used to run a once-a-week course called Relaxation for Positive Change. This course was very popular. Very quickly, it became known as The Chill Pill, thus dubbed by a huge African-American basketball player who attended religiously every week.

Initially, I felt uneasy about *The Chill Pill* mainly because we didn't do anything! There was no psychology, no analysis, no therapy, no motivational talk, no group work. All we did was breathe, meditate, relax, be still, enjoy the silence and let go. That was it! Together we created our own sanctuary—our own on-the-spot monastery—and people simply turned up, tuned in and let go.

The Chill Pill offered people a *breathing space* where they could re-center, re-connect and re-focus. Most of the meditations centered on letting go, i.e., letting go of fear, letting go of struggle, letting go of busyness, letting go of hurry, letting go of self-criticism. I soon started taking requests: "What shall we let go of this week?" Popular subjects included "Stress!", "Anger!",

"Unavailable men!", "Work!", "The boss!" and "Over-seriousness!"

The Chill Pill reached full attendance capacity without any significant promotion or publicity. It attracted all sorts of people, including a doctor, a policeman, a social worker, an opera singer, the director for public health, a head chef of a top hotel, a television presenter and a professional footballer—all of whom came simply to *relax, release and let go.*

People described *The Chill Pill* as "a saving grace", "a dose of sanity" and "a touch of heaven". One person called it her "emotional chiropractic" because she felt so realigned and balanced afterwards. Each week people reported how great insights and inspiration leaped out of the silence. Many people also reported major breakthroughs and shifts in relationships and work. *The Chill Pill* showed me that relaxation really is the greatest psychotherapy.

My work has taught me that *any pain or struggle is a signal to relax and let go.* Pain and struggle are signs you are holding on to a fear, judgment, expectation, doubt or some other self-limiting thought. They are signs that your best thinking is not working for you. Pain and struggle are evidence that a better way will reveal itself to you if you will first let go.

The beauty of letting go is, *you stop thinking!* First God created man; man then created thought; and ever since there has been nothing but trouble! Face it, nothing has got you into more trouble than your own thoughts. Your thoughts do not always live up to their billing. When you let go, you clear your mind, you make space, you open up, you receive inspiration.

The best things in life happen when you dare to let go! How good is romance when you let go and trust! How great is sex when you let go and join! How attractive are you when you let go and relax! How effective at work are you when you let go and give yourself fully! Letting go inspires creativity, intimacy, laughter, balance, abundance and peace. How often, then, do you really let go?

"Suffering is attachment; happiness letting go," said the Buddha, who created a whole doctrine around the principle of letting go. In more recent times, Alcoholics Anonymous have made famous the slogan, "Let go, let God". This is a great challenge for a generation of dysfunctionally independent people who are too afraid to trust in anything other than their own thoughts.

Letting go plays a part in every healing. It is also the key to sustainable success in relationships, work and life. The most successful people I know make time every day for a breathing space, healing interludes, meditation and letting go. Every day make space for something other than your own everyday thoughts. Make space for something higher.

Practice letting go of your ego every day. When you breathe out, let go of your ego; and when you breathe in, open up to your Unconditioned Self. Consciously imagine yourself tuning in to God, to heaven and to the highest in you. When you feel calm and centered, ask these two questions: 1) *What shall I let go of today?*, and 2) *What shall I open up to today?* Listen. Be guided. Let yourself go.

WHAT YOU TRY TO CONTROL, YOU CAN RUIN

Have you ever noticed that what you try to control the most often gives you the most grief!

Some "things" require control. Some "things" like traffic control, pest control, crime control and bladder control are all very helpful. Control is not, however, the answer to everything. In fact, with relationships, creativity, healing and happiness, for instance, holding on to control is often a major block to success.

The relationships you try to control the most are the ones that suffer the most. Control is fear. Trying to control the people you love betrays old wounds, old heartbreaks and old pain. Control does not make a relationship safe. On the contrary, control kills trust, intimacy, romance, spontaneity and growth. You cannot control unconditional love. You have to give up control (and fear) to win love.

Control in relationships often causes power struggles, disenchantment and unhappy endings. Whenever you try to change someone, you are trying to control them. Whenever you try to make choices for another person, you are also trying to control them. Your relationship is no longer about love and respect; it is about manipulation and dominance. A power struggle will emerge, there will be a war, both parties will lose – unless control is relinquished.

We are a generation who have been sold beliefs like "control is power", "control is strength", "control is freedom". "Get control of your life" is a very popular mantra in our society. Control is healthy if it means taking responsibility for your life, choosing your thoughts and being focused. But control can also be misused. Too much control can make you inflexible, defensive, shortsighted and ineffective.

Relinquishing control is often the first step to greater creativity, inspiration and healing. It takes courage, though. I remember once a very famous singer asked me for some relationship counseling, but only on the strict condition that I did not ask her any questions about her parents, her ex-husband or her private life! Alas! *Trying to control your own healing is one of the most common blocks to wholeness and happiness.*

Control often causes a mind cramp that kills creativity, innovation and progress. In recent years, I have worked closely with the leading new wave managers who are evolving their companies beyond the old-fashioned "command and control cultures" that did so much to stifle proactivity and success. These highly successful people understand the value of continually letting go of old plans, pictures and policies for something better.

Control often betrays an attempt to "do" life all on your own. It smells of ego, close-mindedness, fear of change, even fear of success. Too much control can block receiving, partnership, synergy and growth. Too much control can cut you off from a better idea, new ways, extra help and more abundance. Too much control can leave you hemmed in by your own little thoughts so that you lose sight of the big picture.

How do you know if you are applying too much control? Simple. Your life will not be working for you. Where there is too much control, there will be no flow, no abundance, no joy. Control is the *Achilles' heel* you drag behind you as you wade through struggle, conflict and pain. Pain is always a control issue. Whenever you are in pain, you are being asked to give up some control somewhere.

Essentially put, too much control leaves you playing small. It disconnects you from your Unconditioned Self. It stunts your growth. Creativity is constipated. Your options are limited. You are left playing with the devil you know. You miss the higher ground. By contrast, the prizes for letting go of control include new growth, new adventures and new prosperity.

Take a moment now to run a control check on your life. Notice the relationships and situations where you are applying too much control. *Control usually conceals fear*, i.e., fear of loss, hurt, failure, etc. Identify your fear. Ask yourself, *"Is this fear a fact or is it just a fear?"* Recognize that control will not resolve these fears. If anything, too much control accentuates fears.

Wherever you are applying too much control, ask yourself, *"What would work better than control here?"* Could you perhaps communicate more, trust more, open up more, laugh more, or ask for extra help? Be open to a better way. Affirm "God is in charge here", or something similar, so as to make yourself available for the highest possible outcome in every relationship, every endeavor and every moment.

TRUST CAN TRANSFORM EVERYTHING

This is a story of fear and trust.

had just finished an excellent lunch on board a flight to Amsterdam. I was on my way to give a one-day seminar with psychologist Dr. Wayne Dyer called *Manifesting Abundance*. I sat back in my chair, closed my eyes and smiled. I felt relaxed and happy, and I was genuinely looking forward to meeting Wayne and the seminar delegates. "All is well," I mused.

Without warning my stomach rolled over, my blood pressure dropped, and my mind went into free-fall. All my thoughts were ablaze with fear. Gasping for breath, I searched through my hand luggage. Twice. I found nothing! My ego was staring certain death in the face. The unthinkable had happened. I had forgotten my notes for my talk!

I watched my thoughts for the next few minutes as I continued to fly through a turbulent mind-space of fear, blame and worry. I did not try to control this panic. I simply let it fly. Because I did not resist the panic, it soon ran out of fuel. And then a beautiful thought occurred to me: "What if it is in everyone's highest interest that you let this talk be spontaneous and without plan?" Now I felt fear and excitement.

When I walked on to the stage in Amsterdam, my ego was standing to my left and God was standing to my right. On the one hand, I was worried that I had nothing to give, and on the other hand, I was willing to trust that if I gave up control and let go then something bigger than my fear would take charge. After all, inspiration abhors a vacuum.

That day I gave one of the best talks of my life. I received a standing ovation. All my books sold out in thirty minutes flat. I received four invitations to give future talks. My trust had transformed what looked like a disaster into an experience of new creativity and powerful learning. "All is well," I remembered.

Trust takes you past fear. It is the "miracle ingredient" that makes for success in relationships and work. Trust in relationships can inspire new levels of intimacy, communication and love. It can heal conflict, facilitate forgiveness and turn enemies into friends. Trust at work can inspire great vision, creativity, motivation and teamwork. Trust is very powerful.

What is trust? There are two levels. First, *trust is intention.* It is where you place your focus, energy and belief. In other words, *where you place your trust is where you place your power.* Hence, when trust is one-pointed and one-minded, it can be very dynamic and creative. Second, *trust is joining.* It takes you beyond your ego, beyond fear, into whole new reaches of creativity, inspiration and synergy. This is where one plus one equals three.

Trust can also be a philosophy. Some of the most talented and creative people I know—artists, entrepreneurs, business leaders, healers—live by the power of trust. They trust, for instance, that all things are possible. They trust in God. They trust in love. They trust in honesty. They trust in themselves. They trust in the goodness of others. Their trust is their strength.

You never lack trust. A client of mine once said about his new business venture, "I have 100 per cent trust: 40 per cent trust in fear; 30 per cent trust in self-doubt; 20 per cent trust in certain failure; 9 per cent trust in something going wrong; and 1 per cent trust in lots of hope!" You always have trust. The key is to know where you are placing your trust.

When you are afraid, it is a sure sign you are trusting in your own ego. To the ego trust feels like walking the plank. It is a death march. This is because trust takes you past your ego's perceptions to a field of greater possibilities. Trust invokes the highest in you. It gives you access to the unlimited potential of your Unconditioned Self. With trust, all things are possible.

Review your life for a moment. With every relationship and work project ask yourself, "*Where am I placing my trust?*" and "*What is my intention here?*" and "*What am I really committed to here?*" Remember, where you place your trust is where you place your power. Be willing to go beyond your ego. Let God inspire your work today. Let love bless your relationships today. Let the highest in you illuminate your thoughts today. Trust fully in good things happening today to you and everyone.

OLD DEFENSES BLOCK
NEW SUCCESS

Every defense is really a fear which forces you to play small, live in lack, and limit what is really possible. Thus, no defense can make you strong, no defense can win you freedom, and no defense can show you your true power.

Angela was a lawyer, single, in her late thirties. She was a large woman with a large body, large persona, large aura and large laugh. She was very funny, very quick, very intelligent and very cynical. One side of Angela was warm, feminine and strong, the other side was abrupt, intellectual and brittle. She oscillated between being open and closed, positive and cynical, willing and defensive.

"You look far too young to be of any help to me," said Angela when she first came to me for help.

"Would you like to come back in ten years' time?" I asked.

"Can you guarantee you won't have put your charges up?" she countered.

"No," I said. I offered Angela a cup of tea.

"No, let's not waste time," she said.

"Okay then, why are you here?" I asked.

Angela's exact answer was, "Well, the new man in my life is far too nice and I don't know what to do about him."

Angela had recently fallen in love. "I did not mean to fall in love. It's all very inconvenient," she said. The last time Angela had really fallen in love was over ten years ago. "I've been a career woman ever since," she said. Angela told me that the first two months with "my Prince Charming" had been wonderful. "It was like a fairy tale," she said. The last couple of weeks, however, had not been so good.

"I've lost the plot," said Angela. "It's like I'm a teenager going through menopause. I'm happy, in love, acting like a bitch and pushing him away." Angela talked of her need for rules and healthy boundaries. I explained that rules and boundaries often hide old fears, old pain and old wounds. Angela then told me about a string of abusive relationships she had in her twenties. "I thought I had healed all that," she said. "No, you just got busy," I said.

Angela's fearful beliefs about love and romance were not current. They were at least ten years past their sell-by date. "Maybe I am too cynical for love," she once said. "Cynicism is not your true nature," I suggested. Angela was using cynicism as a defense against her old unhealed pain. Ultimately, she would have to choose between cynicism and love, the past or freedom.

Angela wavered for several weeks between saying "Yes" or "No" to her Prince Charming. On a deeper level, she was deciding whether, a) to believe in love again, or b) to accept she was worthy of this much love. Angela's mind was like a busy racetrack with hurdles and horses called "Old Beliefs About Men", "New Possibilities", "Self-Doubt", "I'm in Love" and "Is This Okay?" Every week the lead changed hands. Neck and neck the horses raced for victory. It was touch and go, but "New Possibilities" finally came through.

After her last big heartbreak, Angela had decided never to get hurt again. She went about defending herself to the hilt. She built herself a castle with big walls, pulled up the drawbridge, drained the moat and burned the bridges. Occasionally, she would spy potential suitors from her ivory tower, but that was all. Angela was safe and lonely, safe and unhappy, safe and unfulfilled. Her defenses had failed her.

The thing about defenses is, *defenses don't really work*. A defense is a wound. It can't get you what you really want, and it usually attracts the very thing you are trying to avoid.

Defenses preserve the ego without healing it. Think for a moment, "*Who is the most defensive person I know?*" How happy are they? How free are they? How fulfilled are they? Here is the folly of defensiveness:

> Fear attracts fear—it does not attract love.
> Cynicism begets cynicism—it cannot bring hope.
> Control is manipulative—it cannot gain trust.
> Independence is for itself—it denies intimacy.
> Blame causes problems—it is not a solution.
> Attack provokes attack—it cannot win safety.
> Anger stirs guilt—it cannot make peace.
> Denial makes for deception—it denies truth.
> Avoidance is amiss—it shirks growth.
> Dishonesty is a lie—it cannot support healing.
> Hiding is dishonest—it cannot set you free.

Defenses are meant to build you up, but often they make you weak. Ask yourself, "*Who is the most defenseless person I know?* " How happy are they? How abundant are they?

Defenselessness is very powerful. Defenselessness is also a great healer. When you let go of old defenses, old pain lets go of you; when you let go of fear, fear lets go of you; when you let go of cynicism, cynicism lets go of you; when you let go of attack, attack lets go of you.

Make an inventory of all your old defenses. Note the relationships and situations where you are most defensive. Notice how your defenses don't make you happy. Be willing to let go of the old defenses, old fears and old wounds that are past their sell-by date. Picture yourself communicating differently, thinking differently and acting differently. Be open to new possibilities.

WHEN YOU TAKE A STEP,
A BRIDGE APPEARS

Imagine that right now you have reached a point in your life where you are being asked to, "Take the next step". What does that step look like?

In the film *Indiana Jones and the Last Crusade* there is a scene where Indiana, played by Harrison Ford, stands at the edge of a chasm that drops to forever. On the other side of the chasm is the Holy Grail—a symbol for all God's treasures. There appears to be no way across the chasm. Time is of the essence. Further, the audience has finished all the popcorn and the closing credits are about to roll!

Indiana consults an old parchment to consider his next step. It shows an ancient figure walking on air across the chasm. "This must be a leap of faith," Indiana says. Meanwhile, his feisty father, played by Sean Connery, implores his son, "You must believe." Indiana takes the next step. He steps out on to what looks like thin air and his foot finds a bridge waiting for him. Brilliant! With one step, the Holy Grail is now in reach.

I often refer to this scene in my seminars. Occasionally, someone will point out it is only a story! This is true. However, it more than capably illustrates a universal truth which is, *when you step forward, your life moves on.* If Indiana Jones had waited for a bridge to appear before taking a step he would have waited forever. The bridge was already there. He just had to take a step to see it.

Taking the next step in your life is all about trust and faith. The power of faith is that it takes you beyond the edge of your own perceptions into a whole other world of new possibilities. Faith is the bridge that takes you from fear to freedom, old to new, past to present, lack to abundance, ego to God. Faith is a great adventure.

"What if you take a step and there is no bridge?" This question reveals a person's faith. Cynics fear they have burned all their bridges. They no longer believe in bridges so they see no bridges. Believing is seeing! By contrast, optimists know *there is always a bridge.* Either that, or, they will learn to fly! Each next step takes you somewhere.

Life is full of Indiana Jones steps. Personally, I never feel completely ready to write a new book. The key is to begin.

Without an Indiana Jones step there would be no art, no poetry, no symphonies, no film scripts, no innovation, no genius, no discovery, no new relationships, no adventure.

Love is full of Indiana Jones steps. Asking someone out on a date is an Indiana Jones step. Saying "Yes" is also an Indiana Jones step. Opening your heart to love again is an Indiana Jones step. So too is commitment, trust, marriage, intimacy, co-habiting, recommitment, parenthood, etc. I have not met anyone who felt completely ready for parenthood. You learn as you go.

One step is all it takes to find your bridge—one "Yes", one act of courage, one radical thought, one shift in perception, one dare, one prayer, one moment of forgiveness, one apology, one phone call. Remember, you are the alchemist. The world mirrors your intention, your trust and your faith. Either you can wait, or, you can start walking.

Unless you choose happiness,
you will wait forever for it.
Unless you bring a new intention,
the outcome will be the same.

Unless you let go of your past,
you will not see the present.
Unless you drop your defenses,
you will never reach safety.
Unless you first commit to her,
you will not see her beauty.
Unless you first commit to him,
he cannot be the one.
Unless you are ready to love,
you will not find love.
Unless you give up your ego,
you will not discover your spirit.

Imagine there is a place in you of perfect wholeness, perfect wisdom and perfect peace. Step into this place now. This is your Holy Grail. Take guidance here as you ask, "*What is the next step?* " in your relationships, your work and your spiritual journey through life. Remember, you need not make this step alone. You can picture someone who inspires you walking with you. If you get no clear guidance, be open to taking a next step anyway. Even openness is a next step.

WHAT ARE YOU WAITING FOR?

There once was a man who waited all his life to be happy. The last anyone heard of him, he was still waiting.

Do you ever find yourself sitting in life's Waiting Room, killing time, waiting for happiness, waiting for the big love, waiting for the green light, waiting for better times, waiting for your bridge to appear? What are you really waiting for: courage—permission—your turn—zero risk—the right moment—a sign—a guarantee?

Are you waiting or are you stalling? Is your waiting game really necessary or are you secretly afraid to commit, to participate and to risk giving yourself? Sometimes waiting is a cover for fear, self-doubt, unworthiness and not taking responsibility for your life.

"*The WAIT Problem*" is a common block to happiness, love and success. In fact there is no need to wait. Happiness awaits you. Love awaits you. Success awaits you. They await your choice, your acceptance, a sign from you, a "Yes" from you. For as long as you wait, you cannot see what is already possible, what is already here, and what is already waiting for you.

The WAIT Problem is really a disconnect between what is truly possible and what you will let yourself receive. Symptoms of *The WAIT Problem* include limbo, lack, feeling stuck, no flow, no synchronicity, more procrastination, over-analyzing, no inspiration, no energy, and deadness. Your life is on hold because you are. The world is waiting because you are.

It is ironic that we live in a society which hates to wait, stand in line, or be put on hold for anything—any "No Waiting" sign is guaranteed a sale—and yet *The WAIT Problem* is most prevalent. Here are some examples of *The WAIT Problem*:

Relationships suffer because people wait for things to get good before they fully commit; they wait for the right signs instead of signing up.

People are lonely because they wait for love instead of being loving; they wait for friendship instead of being a friend.

At work, one of the biggest causes of poor team spirit is that everyone waits for the team spirit to get better.

People age prematurely because they wait to have fun after work, after chores, after bills, after this year, after retirement, after the grandkids are settled.

Healing takes longer because people wait to be well again before they choose happiness, wellness and love. Choose now.

Silly conflicts last forever because two people wait to get what they will not give. Each waits for the other to make the first move.

Exhaustion, illness and failure happen because people wait to achieve success first before they meditate, rest and balance their life.

People struggle because they wait for life to get better before they give up struggle; they wait for peace instead of choosing peace.

The perfect antidote to waiting is willingness. Willingness is the great invocation, the philosopher's stone, and pure alchemy. Willingness harnesses the power of intention, trust, faith and commitment. Willingness makes for new possibilities.

Willingness inspires readiness. With readiness all things are possible. The spiritual aphorism, *when the student is ready the teacher appears*, can also be extended to include, when the lover is ready a partner appears, when the artist is ready inspiration appears, when you are ready opportunity appears, and, as my friend and workshop leader, Chuck Spezzano says, "When the receiver is ready, the gift appears."

Be ready and let yourself receive. Be ready and let yourself be guided, be helped, be inspired, be blessed and be loved. Be ready and be willing, for the truth is that nothing moves in this world without your willing it.

THERE ARE NO HAPPY PERFECTIONISTS!

A true perfectionist is someone who sees everything in a perfect light. He is the mystic who trusts that life unfolds perfectly. She is the witness who watches the world mirror your every belief. He is the healer who sees your true wholeness. She is the lover who knows you are perfect love.

People who call themselves perfectionists are not usually this happy. On the contrary, they are perfectly miserable. They suffer constant inquisition and torture at their own hands. They are racked by impossibly high self-standards. They crucify themselves with taunts of criticism, inferiority and lack. And then they bury themselves alive with self-recrimination. Above all, there is no self-acceptance, no compassion, no kindness and no happiness now.

So-called perfectionists are always getting ready to be happy, but are never completely ready. They are in constant preparation, always working at and striving after happiness, instead of *being happy*. They are always searching for the perfect love, instead of *being loving*. They have a plan for everything—

and the plan never works. In truth, they are stalling on what they say they want.

Perfectionists are terrible *musterbators*. They have a secret file full of self-imposed conditions—"musts", "oughts" and "shoulds"—that absolutely *must* come first before anything. For example, to be happy, "I must have a reason", "I must deserve it", "I must be good", "I must be perfect", "I must be in a relationship", "I must have no cellulite", "I must be doing something", "Everything must be perfect", "Everyone must like me", and "Everyone must be happy first".

Perfectionists are too busy musterbating to be in love. Their romances are usually short-lived epics full of fantasy, pedestals and arrows through the heart. They place too many conditions on love. For example, their perfect partner must be the right height, the right shape, have the right hair color, and be the right age. Also, they must be permanently happy, never needy, have no flaws, and be totally enlightened. Of course, all these conditions are a perfect cover for massive self-doubt, fear of intimacy, and fear of love.

A perfectionist musterbates at work from nine to five. The internal memos read, "I must not make a mistake," "I must not fail", "I must dot every 'i' ", "I must cross every 't' ", "I must be right about everything" and "I must get everything done". The perfectionist tries to compensate for raging self-doubt with painstaking effort, excessive control, unnecessary rigidity and other self-defeating behaviors. Nothing is good enough because they project "I am not good enough" on to everything they do.

Do you ever musterbate? What do you insist *must* happen first before you can be happy? What *must* happen first before you have inner peace? What *must* happen first before you can enjoy perfect self-acceptance? Take a moment now to complete the following sentences. Say each sentence ten times, and write down any "must" that springs to mind.

> "To be happy I must . . ."
> "To feel good about myself I must . . ."
> "To be really successful I must . . ."
> "To be loved I must . . ."
> "To love my partner they must . . ."

Whenever you are struggling, in pain, stalling, feeling lost or giving yourself a hard time, you are probably musterbating over something.

Perfectionists are sad clowns. They juggle with conditions and rules that are not real. They fall over impossible standards and land flat on their face. They chase after happiness instead of letting their inner happiness bubble up. They seek the perfect partner instead of being the perfect partner. They are blind to their own perfection. They do not see their own beauty, wholeness and wonder.

Perfectionism is a sham. It is self-attack dressed up as "high standards"; it is the ego masquerading as nobility; it is fear and unworthiness fronting as something heroic. It is a personal hell that teases you with promises that are never met. Every time you let go of a "must", a condition or a rule, you step closer to perfect, unconditional happiness. Every time you let go of your own perfect plan, you make space for something greater.

BE UNREASONABLE!

Here is a thought that is eccentric and divine, and that one day might save your life: *happiness needs no reason!*

Shortly after my book *Laughter the Best Medicine* was published, I did an interview with local disc jockey Gordon Astley for BBC Radio. I knew Gordon very well. For two years I did a "Stress Busters Phone-in" on his popular morning show. Together we agreed that instead of a normal interview, we would try an experiment—"The Unreasonable Happiness Experiment".

At 10.59a.m., Gordon told his listeners, "After the news, I will prove to you *it is possible to be happy for no reason at all.* Stay tuned!" He then switched to the news desk. When Gordon came back on air he began, "They say it's the best medicine . . ." He then paused for one, two, three seconds before, completely unannounced, he ran a tape of the most blissful belly laughter you have ever heard.

The tape was of a man laughing solo for forty-five seconds. It began softly with gentle chuckles, expanded into a hearty chortle, and climaxed on a crescendo of uncontrollable guffawing. It was totally infectious. Go to www.happiness.co.uk to hear it for yourself. Gordon, myself, his producer and the weather girl laughed "unreasonably". It was a moment of pure joy. But it didn't stop there.

For the next hour, the phone lines were jammed with callers expressing thanks for "The Unreasonable Happiness Experiment". We received calls from everyone, including a teacher, a doctor, a florist, a bank manager and a clown. "Happiness needs no reason," said one caller. "I have always said "Happiness is in the heart," said another. "Happiness is free, and a good laugh costs nothing," said another. "Thanks for reminding me to laugh," said another.

The final call was from a woman who sounded depressed and lonely. "Do you really believe in *unreasonable happiness*, Robert?" I told her that most days I remember happiness needs no reason, love needs no reason and kindness needs no reason, but I also have days when I forget too. The woman then said, "I am having one of those days today. I just couldn't see a reason to be happy. But now I'm thinking maybe I don't need a reason."

The highest truth is, *you do not need a reason to be happy.*

Your ego will disagree with this, however, because ego uses "reasons" as its chief currency for being, doing and giving. Everything must have a reason according to ego, i.e., "*I will be happy if . . .*" and "*I will be happy when . . .*" and "*I will be kind if...*" and "*I will love you when . . .*"

Unreasonable happiness is natural to infants who smile for no reason, laugh for fun and play for play's sake. Unreasonable happiness is also natural to your Unconditioned Self. True happiness needs no reason, no special equipment (i.e., money!), no perfect moment, no permission, no justification and no ideal circumstance. *Being happy* is about folding back into something already innate in you.

Can you still do it? Do you ever kick back and let yourself laugh for no reason? Do you ever smile the unreasonable smile? Do you ever let yourself be surprised by joy? Are you ever unashamedly spontaneous? Do you still love unconditionally without reason, expectation or demand? Can you ever be happy *just because*? Try it!

Be still for a moment and meditate on *unreasonable joy*. See if you can let your innate joy bubble up for no good reason. Dial direct to your Unconditioned Self, and surrender to the thought of *unreasonable joy*—no striving, no earning, no deserving, no reason necessary. *Reasons, conditions and rules are really covert resistance to joy, innocence and being unconditional again.*

Experiment today with being more unreasonable than usual. Remind yourself how easy it can be to choose joy, choose love and choose kindness. Here are some suggestions to start you off:

- Be unreasonably kind to yourself today.
- Kiss your partner for no reason at all.
- Smile the unreasonable smile at work.
- Call a friend for no specific reason.
- Send flowers to a friend, just because.
- Choose to have a great day, regardless.
- Meditate on unreasonable joy today.
- Dress up, eat out, your treat, no reason.
- Let no reason stop you being you today.

The more unconditional you are with yourself, *and with others*, the easier it is to remember that in truth there is no good reason not to be loving, not to be kind and not to be joyous. Be unreasonable!

TRUE ASSERTIVENESS IS A "YES"

"Yes" is the secret to success, to love and to everything you really want.

When Monica received an invitation to her school reunion, "Graduates of '76", it triggered what she described as "an enormous midlife crisis and depression". Two weeks later, she made her first appointment to see me.

"I want to go to the reunion, but I'm terrified," said Monica.

"Why?" I asked.

"Well, I'm nearly forty for heaven's sake," she said, looking very worried.

"Correct me if I'm wrong," I said, "but won't everybody else be nearly forty too?"

"Yes," she laughed, "but I haven't done anything with my life. Once I was twenty-one, then twenty-two, then twenty-three and now I'm thirty-eight all of a sudden! And I haven't got a life!"

Monica told me, "My grief is that I have no romance, no

husband, no children, and time is running out." In her twenties, Monica had been a fashion model working in New York, Paris and London. "I was young and naïve and made bad choices with men," she said. "I was two-timed, date-raped, ripped off and exploited. Eventually, I learned to be more assertive, to say "No", and to protect myself."

When Monica told me, "I still haven't found Mr. Right," I explained, "That's because you haven't been truly assertive."

"What do you mean?" she asked.

"Well, you have said "No" to being abused; but you haven't said "Yes" to being loved. You have said "No" to being naïve again; but you haven't said "Yes" to being loving again."

"Yes, you're absolutely right," said Monica.

Monica was also depressed about her exhausting work schedule. "I swore that when I quit modeling I would never work this hard again, but here I am again with no social life, no time out and no holidays."

Once again I said, "You haven't been assertive enough."

"How so?" she asked.

"Well, you said "No" to burnout; but you didn't say "Yes" to balance. You said "No" to sacrifice; but you didn't say "Yes" to fulfillment."

I told Monica I was going to prescribe her a course of "Yes" meditations.

"What, you mean like "Yes" to tall, dark, handsome, wealthy, intelligent men with no kids and no baggage?" she laughed.

"Be more unconditional," I said. "Simply say "Yes" to love, to balance, to happiness, and then let God take care of the details."

I asked Monica to meditate every morning on everything she really wanted to say "Yes" to. The first week didn't go well.

"I didn't have much time," Monica said.

"That's your resistance speaking," I said.

"But I was busy," she said.

"That's your unworthiness speaking," I said. Monica admitted she felt uneasy about asking for what she really wanted. " 'Yes' is harder than 'No'," she said.

I encouraged Monica in her meditation to let every in-breath be a symbol of her willingness to receive and say "Yes", and to let every out-breath be a symbol of her willingness to let go of her resistance and unworthiness. Eventually Monica's morning "Yes" meditations took the form of a prayer which she gave me a copy of. It read:

Dear God,
I say "Yes" to love today.
Help me to give and receive love.
I say "Yes" to happiness today.
Help me to enjoy each moment.
I say "Yes" to balance today.
Help me to relax and smile.
I say "Yes" to me today.
Help me listen to my heart.
I say "Yes" to miracles today.
I say "Yes" to life today.

Monica came to see me one week after her school reunion. She had had a great time. "I don't know what I was so worried about," she said.

"That's great," I said.

"And guess what?" she said, laughing like a schoolgirl, "I got asked out on a date by an old classmate."

"What did you say?" I asked.

"I said 'Yes' of course!" replied Monica.

"Yes" is pure intention. It is the key to choice, purpose and assertiveness. "Yes" is also the key to healing. For instance, when you are unhappy, honor it and say "Yes" to healing. When you are struggling, notice it and say "Yes" to greater ease. When you are afraid, breathe with it and say "Yes" to help. When you are in pain, don't resist it, just say "Yes" to peace. And when you are at your wits' end, simply let go and say "Yes" to a new beginning.

COMMIT TO HAPPINESS NOW!

Some things never change: your greatest opportunity for healing and happiness has been, will be, still is, NOW!

My most prized possession is my "Happiness NOW" wristwatch. I designed it myself as a gift for my own thirty-fifth birthday. It is a gold-plated watch, with a stainless steel case back, a mineral glass lens, a black leather strap and a white watch dial with black lettering in a classic roman font. In the center it reads "Happiness". And instead of the normal numbers "one" to "twelve", it reads "NOW" twelve times.

Within a month of my birthday, I had over fifty unsolicited orders for a replica "Happiness NOW" watch from friends, colleagues and clients. Everyone I showed my watch to said, "I really need one of those." One friend who is a doctor said my watch should be made available on prescription—as an aid to mental health and inner wellbeing.

I made my "Happiness NOW" watch as a reminder to slow down, be present and enjoy the moment more often. All my life, I have been plagued by "fast genes"—i.e., a belief that happiness is a chase, a dash and a pursuit, as opposed to a choice and a surrender. I often catch myself living life fast—too fast to enjoy happiness now. Judging by the orders for my watch, I am not alone.

In heaven, I believe all the clocks and watches tell exactly the same time always: "NOW". When I meditate, I experience an infinite "NOW" that is beyond time. "NOW" is another name for God. "NOW" is another name for Heaven. "NOW" is another name for joy. "NOW" is where you get to leave your ego behind and meet your whole Self.

How do you know if you are living in the now? The answer is, *you are happy*! Since time began, spiritual teachers have taught their students to live in the "here and now", to "enjoy the moment", and to "seize the day". And since time began, spiritual students have repeatedly disregarded their teacher's wisdom at first. Like the Prodigal Son, we all eventually return to "NOW" to find our spiritual home.

Living in the "not now" is a chief cause of unhappiness, pain and lack. The strain of being not present in your own life is simply too great. When you miss out on the present, you miss out on so much. No now; no life. Classic symptoms of living in the "not now" include:

No joy. When you disconnect from "now", it is like hanging up on yourself. You feel lost.

No prosperity. You are in lack because all your investments are tied up in some imagined future.

No rest. You are too busy chasing happiness to be happy.

No being. You are too busy looking for love to be loving.

No peace. You are too anxious "futurizing" and "pasturizing" to enjoy the moment.

No intimacy. You are not present long enough for any real intimacy. Your relationships suffer.

No synchronicity. Whenever you are not fully present, there will be no flow, and you will struggle.

No inspiration. How can you be open to something if you are not present to receive it?

No time. If you don't have the moment, you don't have the time—now, or ever!

No healing. If you save up your best for when life gets better, it never will. Commit to happiness now.

Whenever you decide to be fully present, you unlock the door to happiness now. Make a decision today to commit to happiness NOW. Commit to loving your partner even more today, and watch how beautiful he or she becomes. Commit to enjoying your work even more today, and watch how much fun it can be. Commit to being grateful for your life today, and watch how your gratitude grows. Shift happens whenever you commit yourself to happiness now!

YOU ARE NEVER STUCK,
JUST AFRAID

I once had a client who described her problem as "un-flushable".

"I keep pulling the chain, and it keeps coming back again," she said.

"Sounds like a real stinker," I said.

This made her smile. "I feel so stuck," she said.

"That must be frightening," I said.

"Yes it is, because I just can't seem to move on," she said.

"Can't or won't?" I asked.

Over the years, I have met hundreds of clients who complained of ruts, vicious circles, dead ends and brick walls. Their life was at a sticking point and no amount of thinking, doing, trying or talking appeared to help. God was apparently not answering mail. The light at the end of the tunnel had blown a fuse. And any silver lining looked tarnished. Now, in desperation, they had come to see me!

One of the most important things I have learned about the "psychology of stuck" is that *being stuck is really a form of self-sabotage.* People who are stuck are usually being held back by a riot of self-attack and self-doubt. The ego is on the rampage, looting the mind of vision, courage and trust. In truth, this anarchic self-attack is really a resistance operation that is fighting the fear of something new.

Whenever you feel stuck, it is a sign you are not in your true power. This is why when you feel stuck, you also feel helpless, frustrated, depressed and angry. Not being in your true power means maybe you are relying on struggle instead of intention, fear instead of faith, control instead of openness, pride instead of help, pushing instead of receiving, impatience instead of trust. Ask yourself, *"What is this stuck feeling trying to tell me?"*

When you feel stuck, the real issue is usually fear. Backstage of any stuck story, the ego is busy writing fear into each new scene. For instance, I once counseled a gifted author who had a dark night of the soul before he went on to write an international bestseller. His dark night was really self-sabotage and resistance against a new level of surrender and creativity.

Another time, I counseled a talented graphic designer stuck in a dead-end job who later went on to create his own successful Internet company. He wasn't really stuck; he was afraid—afraid of new risks, afraid of trusting his talent, afraid of failure and afraid of success. Once he faced his fears, his life became unstuck. He was free.

Being stuck often betrays an inner conflict between "yes" and "no", "want to" and "won't", positive intent and fear. The mind is split between what it wants and what it is afraid to have. For instance, people who say they want a relationship but are stuck in *singles' land* are usually willing and unwilling. Couples who hit a sticky patch in an otherwise great relationship are usually facing and resisting a new level of intimacy and love.

When you feel stuck, the mind is often pulling in two opposing directions. For instance, if you say you want help but can't find any, you must really be saying "Yes" and "No" to help. Why would you say "No" to help? Could it be addiction to struggle—unworthiness (i.e., "I don't deserve help")—fear of trust—pride and independence—fear of happiness?

Another example: if you say you want to be less busy but you are not, you must also be saying "Yes" and "No". Why would you want to say "No" to being less busy? Could it be addiction to stress—fear of doing nothing—fear of valueless-ness—avoiding intimacy in relationships—resisting real inspiration—blocking God?

The real question is not "Why am I stuck?" but "Why am I

choosing to be stuck?" Any answer to this question will reveal a fear, a doubt or a block. Here are some more questions to ask yourself whenever you are stuck:

- What am I afraid of?
- What am I resisting?
- What am I blocking?
- What am I not being honest about?
- What am I not looking at?
- What am I holding on to?
- What am I not saying?
- What am I not giving?
- What am I refusing to hear?
- What am I punishing myself for?
- Why do I want it this way?

Remember, whenever you are stuck, you are being invited to choose peace, choose love, choose success, choose help, choose God and choose your higher mind. Being stuck is a prompt to give away the old and receive the new. It is a call to let go of the past and unwrap the present. It is a call to give up your ego and step into your true light.

THINK LESS, LIVE MORE!

Psychologists estimate that yesterday you thought at least 40,000 thoughts. Try now to remember ten of those thoughts that were really useful!

I was seventeen years old when my mind went missing for a whole twenty-four hours. I was playing cricket at the time. I went into bat against a fearsome, super-fast West Indian player, all of six foot eight inches tall (or was it eight foot six inches!), who speared a delivery at me so quick it kissed me between the eyes before I even moved. I fell to the ground (it was the honorable thing to do!). As I came to I heard church bells ringing and birds singing, just like in the cartoons! And then it really hit me—I had no thoughts!

For the next twenty-four hours I was in heaven. I had no thoughts, no judgments, no fear, no doubts, no worries and no ego. I felt fully present, totally energized, and my mind was crystal clear. When I later went out to bat again, I played fluently with great grace and no inhibition. This feeling of pure awareness and total joy lasted all next day until I began to wonder if something was wrong. Until then, "I had no psychology" and I felt completely alive.

In the musical *Guys and Dolls*, my favorite moment is when Vivian Blaine says to Frank Sinatra, "*The doctor thinks my cold might be caused by psychology,*" and Sinatra says, "*Naah, how does he know you got psychology?*" Have you got psychology? Do you ever suffer from thinking too much?

Most of my clients suffer from psychology. Their *being* is fine; their *thinking* is not. Psychiatric units are full of beautiful people suffering from ugly thinking. The intellectual violence of the ego can be especially devastating when you feel vulnerable or low. Little self-doubts can quickly escalate into full-blown self-abuse and self-attack.

Nothing has caused you more trouble than your own psychology. Nothing has hurt you as much as your own thinking. Nothing is as frightening as the idea that someone could read your mind! Pay attention to your thinking, and you will see that 90 per cent of your thoughts are fears, judgments and worries. If you were to let these thoughts out on to the street most of them would be arrested by lunchtime!

Stop thinking and start living! The fact is, you are only ever held back by your own thinking. Fear, worry and pain are literally "all in the mind". In truth, the only block to unconditional love is *your thinking*; the only block to unreasonable joy is *your thinking*; and, the only block to personal success is *your thinking*.

Thinking is often a major block to healing. Clients who insist on deep analysis and reasoning often make slow progress. Real healing is about surrender, forgiveness, letting go and release. Meditation, breath work, homeopathy, yoga, dance, art and massage, for instance, are all so effective because they bypass thinking.

Happiness happens when you least inspect it! If you over-think happiness you end up miserable. Happiness is innocent and simple; it is not an intelligence test and it requires no special I.Q. In truth, you cannot think yourself all the way to happiness. Psychology can take you only so far because true happiness is, ultimately, the relinquishment of thoughts, theories and theses.

To live well, it is important to cultivate a happy relationship with your thoughts. The following five ideas are a wonderful recipe for sanity and joy:

1. *Your thoughts are not real.* Your thinking is not "reality"; it is an interpretation of reality. No thought has any more authority than what you give it.

2. *All thoughts are passing thoughts.* Thoughts are transient. They are like leaves in the wind. The only thoughts that stay are the ones you hold onto.

3. *You choose your thoughts.* No one else does! You can elect to change any thought. You can also choose whether or not to act on any thought.

4. *Thoughts have no power.* Thoughts are literally electrical mental toys that are powered by you. They have no power of their own.

5. *You do not have to take any of your thoughts seriously.* The Chinese philosopher Lao Tzu said, "As soon as you make a thought, laugh at it."

Once a day lay aside your thoughts. Be still. Close your eyes. Breathe deep. Imagine at the heart of your mind there is no fear, no psychology, no ego and no limits. Imagine pure light. Imagine boundless bliss. Imagine great peace. Let your little everyday thoughts disappear now. Let your mind be wholly healed. Surrender and make way for inspiration, higher vision and love. Think less, love more.

WORRY BLOCKS
TRUE CREATIVITY

Imagine writing an unpleasant letter to yourself, mailing it, receiving it, opening it and then being really upset as you read it. That's what worry is like.

Kevin was twenty-three years old, middle-aged, very worried. He had a haunted look. He had a nervous tremor. He never smiled. For the past ten years he had experienced severe panic attacks. Kevin was escorted to my office by his mother who was very worried about him. All the family were worried about Kevin. When I asked Kevin what he was worried about, he replied, "Everything."

Kevin was "worried sick". When I looked into Kevin's eyes, I could see no light, no joy and no playfulness. So I asked him what he did for fun.

"I watch films," he said.

"What are your top five favorite films?" I asked.

Without hesitation, he replied, "*Exorcist, Poltergeist, Halloween, Friday 13*[th] and *Nightmare on Elm Street.*" Kevin was clearly not in his right mind. None of us are when we worry.

Every time you worry you make movies in your mind that are full of imagined horror, disaster scenes and unhappy endings. *Fear is the director, producer and writer.* A frightening fiction takes the place of reality. You do not perceive your own best interests. You have no real vision, clarity or perspective.

Worry is a thief. It will try to rob you of your wisdom, your power and your true creativity. It will try to steal your sanity, take away your peace of mind, and make off with your humor. Worry cannot give you anything of value. It is a taker.

Worry is of the ego. It is your ego's greatest pastime. It is a delusion of the "little self". It has no place in your higher mind. Whenever you worry, it is a sure sign you are relying solely on your little ego for safety and inspiration. Your ego uses worry to justify more fear, more defense, more attack and more avoidance.

Worry solves nothing. The fact is, *worry has never once in the whole history of the human race saved the day*. At best, worry is an alarm bell, but no alarm bell ever put out a fire. Worry is not enough. If you are worrying, you are blocking your true creativity. You are not in your true power. There is a better way.

Shift happens whenever you decide to give up worry for something better. For instance:

"*I worry about my children.*" Worry attacks innocence. It affirms fear, danger, weakness and mistrust. Worry won't make a child safe. See your children's wholeness. Teach them about wisdom and love. Be an example of fearlessness. Trust in their goodness.

"*I worry about my friends.*" Worry is not love; it is fear. When you worry about someone, you are sending them a stream of fear, negativity and doubt. You are affirming danger. Instead of worry, wish your friends a beautiful day. Send them your love. Give them a blessing. Pray they may know true joy.

"*I worry about romance.*" The more you worry about finding a partner or keeping a partner, the more needy, controlling, manipulative and demanding you become. How attractive is that? Dedicate all your relationships to love today. Trust in love. Let love inspire you.

"*I worry about my health.*" Some people worry about their health; others commit to being healthy. Worry won't make you fit. On the contrary, enough worry will give you headaches, migraines, stress, ulcers, hypertension and ill-health. Commit to health.

"*I worry about money.*" Worry affirms scarcity and struggle. It inhibits true generosity. It blocks unconditional giving. It resists real receiving. Heal your relationship with money. Give money a beautiful purpose like spreading love, being kind and giving service. Ask God to be your bank manager.

"*I worry about work.*" Worry blocks true creativity. When you worry about a job interview, a presentation, a project or a meeting, you are focusing on outcomes. Focus instead on intention, purpose and what you want to give.

"*I worry about making mistakes.*" What you really worry about is the self-attack that follows mistakes. When you warn a child, "Don't spill that drink!", what happens next? When you tell yourself, "Don't mess this up!", what do you do? Mistakes are part of life; commit then to forgiveness, humor and learning from them.

"*I worry about my age.*" Worry is self-attack. In truth, no one will hold your age against you if you don't. Remember, you are never too old to love, to smile, to give a compliment, to think positively. Be ageless today. Let your inner light shine today.

"*I worry about the future.*" Worry is a waste of time. It kills spontaneity, fun and happiness now. Commit to now. Give your best to this day. Bless your past. And put the future in God's hands.

"*I worry about dying.*" Worry is a killer. People who worry about dying are usually afraid to live. Whenever you worry, ask yourself, "*What am I avoiding right now?*" Say "Yes" to today. Say "Yes" to what's most important to you. Say "Yes" to life.

ANGER ALWAYS HIDES A GIFT

Anger is like a fat, ugly frog that no one wants to kiss. But even a child knows that when you kiss a frog a gift appears.

Helping Michael with his anger was like nursing a wounded lion with a thorn in its paw. Michael was a struggling artist, aged forty-two, living on his own. His latest girlfriend had walked out on him because of his mood swings. She told Michael she would not return unless he finally got some help. Michael was cynical about therapy but he wanted his girlfriend back.

"I don't have an anger problem," Michael told me. He conceded he sometimes lost his cool, got his buttons pushed, had a sharp tongue, raised his voice, had a short fuse and occasionally drank too much, but he hotly denied any anger problem. When I asked Michael to talk about anger, he cross-examined me, "Are you saying I've got an anger problem?"

Feeling angry is not an anger problem; being dishonest about your anger is. Anger turns to acid when it is mixed with shame, denial and defensiveness. Michael's disowned anger was attacking his peace of mind, inflaming his struggle and burning a hole in his relationships. Healing his anger would obviously be a great gift.

Anger is not pretty to look at, but it can get really ugly if you try to avoid it. Common symptoms of disowned anger include ulcers, migraines, heart disease, broken relationships, depression, irrational thinking, heavy drinking, drug addiction (including nicotine), workaholism, unhealthy competition, intellectual cruelty, bitching, bullying, sarcasm, abuse, road rage and violence.

"I have a right to be angry," Michael said when he finally admitted to feeling angry.

"Yes you do," I replied. "And the more honest, non-judgmental and compassionate you can be about your right to be angry, the less it will eat you up." Michael was relieved to know that I was not trying to take his anger away from him. My real goal was, in fact, to help him connect to his true power.

Anger is not wrong, bad, sinful or illegal. It's just not very smart. It can also be very self-defeating. Anger uses Neanderthal technology. It makes the mouth work faster than your mind. It clenches the fist and closes the heart. It helps you win arguments and start wars. It prefers adrenaline to grace, love and humor. Anger empowers your ego, and disconnects you from your heart.

During one session with Michael I asked him, "What would happen if you gave up your anger?"

Michael surprised himself with his answer. "I'm afraid I would lose my drive, my passion and my creativity." Next we had to check if this was a fact or a fear, i.e., a _Fantasy Experienced As Real_. As Michael gradually let go of his anger he was blessed with greater zest, more creativity and a renewed self-confidence.

Every time you suppress anger or try to avoid it you miss a great opportunity to heal your life. _Anger always hides a gift._ Face your anger with compassion and a healing opportunity arises to release fear, bless old wounds, undo pain, stop playing victim, laugh at irrational thoughts, stop trying to control everything, let go of grievances, resign your ego, ask for help, and restore inner peace.

Anger is like the erupting lava on top of a volcano. This lava is pushed to the surface by the exploding magma of fear, old wounds and self-attack. Hence, when you are angry, the real issues are, 1) **Fear**: _"What am I really afraid of?"_; 2) **Old Wounds**: _"What have I not let go of in the past?"_; 3) **Self-attack**: _"Where am I attacking myself?"_; 4) **Core Gifts**: _"What would_ *really help me right now?"* In other words, what would work better than anger right now?

Example 1: Michael was angry that his agent wasn't getting him enough work. 1) **Fear**: "I'm afraid he doesn't think much of my work"; 2) **Old Wound**: "My mother never said she liked my work"; 3) **Self-attack**: "I'm a useless artist and a useless person"; 4) **Core Gifts**: *Forgiveness:* it's time for Michael to heal his relationship with his mother and himself. *Communication:* Michael must talk honestly with his agent.

Example 2: You are angry at your ex-partner for leaving you. 1) **Fear**: "I'm afraid of the future", "I'm afraid of being on my own", "I'm afraid I will not find love again"; 2) **Old Wound**: "I was the last person in my class have a boyfriend"; 3) **Self-attack**: "I am unlovable"; 4) **Core Gifts**: *Self-acceptance:* attacking your ex-partner is a smokescreen that hides a lack of self-love.

Example 3: You are angry at your boss for criticizing you unfairly. 1) **Fear**: "He does not respect me"; 2) **Old Wound**: "I could never please my father"; 3) **Self-attack**: "I can never get anything right"; 4) **Core Gifts**: *Humor:* just because someone throws you a ball it doesn't mean you have to catch it!

Forgiveness: drop the past. *Success:* catch yourself getting things right.

Example 4: You are angry when your child spills a drink. 1) **Fear**: "I'm too tired to cope with this"; 2) **Old Wound**: "I always play the martyr"; 3) **Self-attack**: "I don't deserve help"; 4) **Core Gifts**: *Honesty:* be honest about how you feel before you get totally exhausted. *Abundance:* let go of martyrdom, unworthiness and resistance to receiving help.

The perfect antidote to anger is to affirm, "*I am not a victim of this world.*" Anger is not your best choice. And it is not your true power. Be honest: *anger does not really work.* It costs too much and it does not deliver what you really want. Be willing to let go of your anger and receive a true gift.

DEFENSES KEEP OLD WOUNDS ALIVE

I don't usually make house calls, but in Liam's case I made an exception. Liam was twenty-eight years old, unemployed and diagnosed as agoraphobic. He had not left his home in over two years. He lived in his bedroom. Twice a day he made visits to the bathroom escorted by his mother for extra protection. Otherwise, Liam watched television, surfed the Internet, and took his medicine.

"So when did all this begin?" I asked.

"I don't know." Liam had repressed everything.

"I don't need help," Liam told me. "No one can help me," he insisted. It took me over an hour to help Liam remember what had triggered the agoraphobia. As a teenager, he had played guitar in a rock band. One night, at their biggest gig yet, a man from the crowd leaped on stage and pointed a gun at Liam's head, threatening to blow his brains out.

"What happened next?" I asked.

"He pulled the trigger and the gun went "bang". I fell to

the floor thinking I had been shot. It was a toy gun. The man was evicted by bouncers."

"Then what?" I asked.

"Nothing. I got drunk and pretended it never happened." In other words, Liam suppressed his feelings. "It wasn't even a real gun," he intellectualized.

Liam quit the band before their next live gig. "I lost interest," he rationalized. He later quit going to live concerts. He also began to avoid large, noisy crowds. "I like quieter places," he rationalized. Next, he stopped going out to parties. "I prefer my own company," he rationalized. Pretty soon, Liam noticed he would perspire and palpitate whenever he got ready to leave the house.

Liam's story is a classic case of how a defense can turn into a disease. Agoraphobia was a defense designed to make Liam safe. It was meant to free him from fear, harm and death. Instead, he was afraid of life, isolated from help, and fenced off from the world. His defenses had failed him. They had healed nothing. They had made everything worse.

Defense mechanisms do not heal. At best, they are emotional bandages you wrap around wounds so as to stem the flow of fear and pain. As with physical wounds, you must eventually take off the bandage to allow for healing. Otherwise, the wound becomes septic and pain spreads. Liam's healing began with letting go of the defenses that were keeping his wounds alive. Liam had to learn how to be defenseless, strong and free again.

Empowerment and healing often begin with releasing defense mechanisms like fear, denial, avoidance, suppression, cynicism, anger, control, substance abuse, eating disorders, etc. Defenses buy you space but they do not heal, they do not make you strong and they do not solve your problems. In fact, they can add to your problems if you persist with them.

A defense mechanism protects you from anything that is "too much", i.e., too much fear, too much pain, too much grief, too much stress, and, too much love, too much joy, too much creativity, too much God. A teacher of mine once said, "Man defends himself against fear because he defends himself against God. When you say "Yes" to God, fear will exit."

Defense mechanisms are of the ego. When you defend yourself, you are defending your ego, your fears, your doubts, your imagined weaknesses. *What you defend, you make real*, i.e., the more you defend your ego the more you identify with it and the more you fence yourself off from true spirit, true inspiration and true power.

Defenses are made of fear. When you defend yourself, you become a fugitive on the run from fear. There is an old principle which states, *what you run from you run to.* In A.A. they say, "Your greatest fear is exactly where your alcoholism is taking you." This is true of every defense mechanism, be it cynicism, avoidance, hiding or denial. Fear attracts more fear, not freedom.

It is a myth that defenses make you strong. You cannot be defensive and free. You cannot suppress feelings and feel whole. You cannot hide wounds and feel safe. You cannot shut down and shine. You cannot be cynical and inspired. You cannot build a wall around yourself and connect to God. You cannot side with fear and also be open to love.

Defenses do not empower you. In fact, defenses are often magnets for pain. It is impossible to be defensive and radiant, defensive and fearless, defensive and open, defensive and abundant, defensive and loving. Defenses tie you to your ego; they keep old wounds alive; they block healing; they affirm fear. Defenses are not love. In fact, *defensiveness is the refusal to give love and receive love.*

Defenselessness makes way for true healing, true love and true strength. Take a moment to imagine what it would be like to be completely defenseless. If you feel fear, you are listening to your ego. Keep imagining true defenselessness. When you feel joy, you are listening to your spirit. It is not danger that comes when you lay down your defenses. It is healing. It is joy. It is inspiration. It is freedom.

STRESS IS AN INVITATION TO CHANGE SOMETHING

"What seems to be the problem?" I asked.
"Life," my client muttered.
"Is that all?" I replied.
"Yes," he said.
"Can you be more precise?"
"No—it's just a severe case of life."
"Do you feel stressed?"
"I don't get stressed," he huffed.

The shame of stress is double trouble. It is a trap that blocks healing and causes great pain. I remember soon after my Stress Busters Clinic opened we mailed 5,000 local businesses offering a free in-house Stress Busters seminar. We anticipated a big response because the city was in the middle of an economic slump and times were hard. We received a grand total of two replies.

One reply was from a Senior Occupational Health Nurse of a motor company. She wrote, "My CEO informs me we have no stress problems. Is this a symptom of stress? Thanks anyway!" The other reply was from a Human Resources Officer at a hospital. She wrote, "Yes please, we definitely need it! My only concern is if we call it a "Stress Seminar" those who need it most will be put off."

One common misperception of stress is, *stress is bad*. Stress is certainly a challenge, but it need not necessarily be "bad", "wrong" or "shameful". Stress only becomes "bad" if you handle it "badly" either by burying it, fighting it, blocking it, avoiding it, or lying about it. The key to managing stress is to work with it, not against it.

Stress is a message. It is a personal invitation to make a change for the better. It is an internal memo that reads, "URGENT—look after yourself!" or "HELP—get support!" or "EMPTY—recharge yourself!" or "IMPORTANT—work smart, not harder!" Stress is not a punishment. It is not a weakness. Stress is information. Use it.

Success with stress starts with inner listening. Listen to your stress; don't block it. What is your stress trying to tell you? Listen for information. What is your stress trying to teach you? Be ready to learn something. How is your stress trying to help you? Be open to receive a great gift. It pays to listen fast because otherwise the messages just get bigger and louder.

Being inauthentic is the biggest cause of stress. Whenever you are not true to yourself—to your heart, your values and what is really important—you will get messages. Similarly, when you stop listening to your intuition, your wisdom, your higher mind and to God, you will experience fear and egoism.

The following "Straw into Gold" questionnaire is an aid to inner listening. It is named after an old alchemy principle that encourages you to use everything, even stress, for your highest purpose. *What is your stress really about?*

What is the fear? Stress always operates with its accomplice—fear! Listen to the fear that is driving your stress. Is the fear a fact, or, is it a *Fantasy Experienced As Real?*

Where am I not being authentic? You are not in your true power when you stray from your values or when you try to people-please. Commit to being honest with yourself.

Who am I not being honest with? Who are you avoiding, attacking or playing small with? What are you not saying? Who could you be communicating more honestly with?

What am I not giving? If you are not fully committed or fully present you will experience struggle and dissatisfaction. Often what is missing is what you are not giving.

What am I not receiving? Imagine how much better your life would be if you decided to be a great receiver. Picture how abundant your life would be.

Who can help me? Be open to receiving great support, inspiration and friendship. Drop your pride, and help will appear.

What am I not listening to? There is enough wisdom within you to inspire a whole world. Listen to your intuition. Follow your heart. Dial direct to God. Be open to the highest thought.

What is the lesson here? One of my own favorite mottoes is, *everything is teaching you something*. Be willing to receive a beautiful lesson right now.

How can I be smarter? Maybe you are stressed because you are trying too hard. Be still and rest awhile. Make way for real inspiration. Use less effort and more wisdom.

What is my real goal? Stop looking at the clock, and check your compass. What is your true north? What is your intention? What is real success? Choose now to get back on track.

There is an old saying, "You are as sick as the secrets you keep." Stress is an opportunity to be more honest, more focused and truer to yourself. This is important because stress is often self-attack. Shift happens when you choose to resist nothing and use everything for your highest good.

EXHAUSTION MEANS THERE IS A BETTER WAY

Your eyes have a red marbled effect. You are down to your last nerve. Your heart beats, but only when it can find the time. Your head is auditioning for a part in high anxiety. The thought of being enthusiastic exhausts you. And you are tired of living. Now is, apparently, a great time to make lots of decisions which will affect the rest of your life!

A client of mine, recovering from a burnout, once said, "My problem is that when I have energy I get busy, and when I am tired I make decisions." Exhaustion is not the best time to sort your life out. When exhausted, you are not in your right mind. You make bad choices. For instance, you probably drink espresso to relax, and you probably think insomnia is a great opportunity to get more work done!

In my lectures, I have often used the figure below as an aid to describing the psychology of exhaustion:

OPPORTUNITYISNOWHERE

When exhausted, vision pales, purpose is clouded, worry reigns, thinking is muddled, and there is a downpour of aggression, frustration and pain. Self-attack is high as you conclude, 1) you are powerless; and 2) there is no opportunity for change. Vision can, however, transform miraculously with enough rest, healing and help, so that what once looked like a dead-end now becomes a way out, i.e., *opportunity is nowhere* becomes *opportunity is now here.*

Exhaustion is an opportunity. It is a sign to reconnect to your heart, to end sacrifice, to drop the ego and to let God in. It is a prompt to heal, be nourished, receive and be open to a better way. When exhausted, you have come to the end of a road, and now it is time to go another way. Exhaustion is about new beginnings.

So why are you exhausted? Here are some hints and exercises that will help you reconnect to the vitality and inspiration of your true Unconditioned Self.

Healing unhealthy self-sufficiency. When you try to "do" life on your own, it creates burnout. So, either you can keep pumping yourself full of extra Vitamin C and iron tablets, or you can stop talking yourself out of asking for and receiving help. Connect!

Healing self-attack. You are constantly running yourself down with criticism, judgment and self-attack. What are you attacking yourself for right now? Self-acceptance switches you on to true power.

Letting go of grievances. Holding on to old wounds takes up great energy. It distracts you from your true innocence, freedom and power. Forgiving others sets you free. Forgiveness gives you back your energy.

Give up the "not now". There is nothing more tiring than trying to live in three places at once, i.e., past, present and future. Choose one! By giving your best to now you will receive more.

Hang up old defenses. Your ego has a massive defense budget. It invests all its energy in fear, control, cynicism and other armor. And yet it is when you relax, trust and love that you really radiate.

End sacrifice. Exhaustion is a sure sign you are in sacrifice. Maybe you are giving energy and time, but you are not really giving yourself, hence there is no real intimacy, synergy, exchange or receiving.

Ditch over-seriousness. You were not created to be serious; you were created to shine. When you try too hard, you block flow and you inhibit true creativity. Ask yourself, "*What could I lighten up about now?*"

Be real. Integrity is energy. It connects you to intention, vision and purpose. Resisting your own guidance is exhausting. Keeping up appearances will wear you down. Be true to what is highest in you.

Practice gratitude. Gratitude is a miracle. It raises the dead, heals vision and turns fatigue into energy. Gratitude will jumpstart your batteries. You cannot be fully grateful and tired at the same time.

ILLNESS IS A CALL FOR LOVE

I once made a woman faint. Her name was Christine. She was a client of mine, a single mother, in her late thirties. Five years previously, Christine's husband had left her for another woman. Her previous good health deteriorated rapidly, one illness quickly following another. Her illnesses included migraine attacks, cystitis, a life-threatening kidney infection, anemia, and, most recently, breast cancer.

Christine was ill and angry. In session one, she attacked her ex-husband with a most skillful character assassination. In session two, she hit out at marriage, men and the world. And in session three, she launched into a ferocious self-attack. For forty-five minutes she targeted all her faults, weaknesses and failures. She especially attacked herself for her failed marriage.

Christine's self-attack showed no sign of ceasefire. I decided, therefore, to interrupt her volley with a deliberately provocative question: "*What do you love about yourself?*" I asked. Christine drew breath, rolled her eyeballs, flipped her head and promptly keeled over. Thankfully she regained consciousness quickly, thus alleviating any fear that I had killed my first patient!

"Loving myself is the last thing on my mind," said Christine, still half-dazed. Christine's life plan was: first get well, sort out her life, get a better job, earn more money, raise her daughter, buy her own home, collect her pension, *and then love herself*! Christine began to see that her illnesses were a call for self-love and self-care NOW! She learned that self-love is not a trophy you win for crossing the finishing line; rather, it's the entry card you sign at the starting line. Without self-love you get nowhere and you win nothing.

Imagine being ill and sending yourself flowers with a note which reads, "I love you". Could this ever happen? How well do you treat yourself when you are ill or injured? The ego is often at its most vicious during illness, inflaming *dis-ease* with impatience, irritation, obstinacy, self-neglect and self-attack. This is hardly surprising as most illness is rooted in self-attack.

A most important question to ask yourself when you are ill is, "*What purpose shall I give to this illness?*" What will you make of your illness? Will it be an enemy or a friend—a problem or a gift—a weakness or a chance to grow—a failure or a lesson—a setback or a setup for some breakthrough? It's your choice.

Illness can be a wakeup call. It can be a great opportunity to cleanse the mind, detox the ego, open the heart and re-center. Illness is a chance to be wise, to refocus and to wake up to what is really important in your life. Illness, as a call for love, is about new beginnings, rebirth and a renewed sense of self. You can use illness to be more real and more whole.

What purpose do you give to illness? The following dictum, called *A Call for Love*, hangs on the wall in my office. It is a series of affirmations that I sometimes give to my clients after we have talked about illness and purpose. It reads:

Illness is a call for love:
"Today, I make way for love."
Illness is a call for peace:
"Today, I surrender all thoughts that hurt."
Illness is a call for joy:
"Today, I release every judgment I ever made."
Illness is a call for forgiveness:
"Today, I give up all my old wounds."
Illness is a call to be present:
"Today, I let go of the past and the future."

Illness is a call for wisdom:
"Today, I will listen to my higher self."
Illness is a call for wholeness:
"Today, I will rest in God."
Illness is a call for grace:
"Today, I will receive a healing gift."

Love is a medicine for every sickness. When ill, hand yourself over to love. Hand over all your wounds, your pain, your resistance and your fear. Hand over your judgments, your cynicism, your anger and your grief. Let love bless your thinking. Let love bless your perception. Let love bless your mind. Let love bless your life. Shift happens whenever you choose love instead of something else.

IF YOU ARE ALIVE, YOU NEED HELP!

When a challenge feels too much, it means it is too much for you alone. All you need is extra help.

Clive has climbed mountains all his life. Every other weekend he visits a mountain range somewhere in the world to pit his wits against some massive opposition. Clive is a real loner. He always travels alone and he always climbs solo. For Clive the real high is self-achievement. "To rely entirely on my own wits is the greatest challenge," he says.

One time, on the eve of a trip to France to climb one of Europe's highest mountains, Clive told me how daunted he felt. I said to him, "Why not ask the mountain to help you with your ascent?" Clive roared with laughter. "Make friends with the mountain and ask it for help," I persisted. Clive couldn't stop laughing. He now had two more mountains to climb. The first was talking to a lump of rock. The second was asking for help!

Clive called me immediately after his latest triumph. He told me, "Just before the final ascent my legs packed up. I was going to turn back when I remembered what you said. I stopped fighting the mountain and asked it to help me. I then felt this tremendous surge of energy lift me up and carry me to the summit. I was definitely helped." It is amazing what can happen when you ask for help!

The ultimate fantasy of a DIP—a <u>D</u>ysfunctionally <u>I</u>ndependent <u>P</u>erson—is that you make it to Heaven all on your own. Then at Heaven's Gate a magnificent party is held in your honor at which you receive a *Lifetime Achievement Award* for never having asked for help. It is decreed your epitaph will read, "No one ever helped me". This is as good as it gets for a DIP.

The truth is you win no extra points for not asking for help. In fact, all you get is extra struggle, extra pain, extra burden and extra loneliness—all unnecessary. Living solo, without help, is pride before a fall. It is not wise or clever. On your own, you are destined to mountain-climb over molehills and never reach your true peak. Without help, it is "you against the world" when it could be "you and the world".

If you are alive, you need help! is a motto I made for myself and other DIPs. Asking for help is hardly an IQ test, but it may test your courage. In fact, the only thing between you and unlimited help is your fear of help. So what might you be afraid of ? Here are ten common blocks to asking and receiving help:

- **Rejection**: "What if I ask and they say No?"
- **Old wounds**: "I don't trust people any more."
- **Pride**: "Asking for help is a weakness."
- **Superiority**: "I am above asking for help."
- **Competitiveness**: "Getting help is a failure."
- **Unworthiness**: "I don't want to burden you."
- **Guilt**: "God can help everyone but me."
- **Cynicism**: "They probably can't help anyway."
- **Independence**: "I don't want to owe anyone."
- **Control**: "What if I don't like the help?"

Shift happens when you ask for help *and really mean it*. Intention rules the world. If you really want help you will receive it. If, however, you are asking for help but not receiving any, you are probably blocking help, i.e., you are saying "Yes" and "No" to help. Remember, by asking for help the only thing you can lose is your ego and some pain. What you win is your freedom again.

The best time to ask for help is when you least feel like it. Herein lies the challenge. If you won't ask for help, be clear you are asking for unnecessary struggle and hardship. In effect, you are choosing ego instead of wisdom, separation instead of strength, and pain instead of peace. Help is your answer. You are never alone; help is nearby, just one request away.

The shortest, most powerful prayer in the world is "Help!" Praying for help is really asking your higher mind to be in charge. Choosing your higher mind is like choosing wisdom over fear, inspiration instead of effort, cashmere over cotton, diamonds instead of glass, God over ego, creativity instead of struggle. Asking for help connects you up.

WHEN YOU HIDE YOUR SPIRITUALITY, YOU LOSE YOURSELF

My friend, Nick Williams, tells a great story about an ex-girlfriend, Lisa, who was a top lawyer in London. Lisa's job was all about long hours, heavy workloads, lots of money and high stress. To help stay effective, Lisa took up meditation, but in secret. She didn't tell anyone for fear of possible ridicule.

Lisa meditated under wraps back at her apartment, which she shared with another professional. The covert operation would start as soon as the coast was clear, i.e., when her room-mate went out. One evening her roommate came home early. She tried to enter Lisa's bedroom. The door was locked. "What are you doing, Lisa?" Flustered, Lisa replied, "I'm . . . I'm masturbating!" This, to Lisa, was less embarrassing than admitting to meditating!

Here is another great story. My brother, David, gave up a prestigious job in London's financial district to help me co-direct The Happiness Project. For ten years, David had worked in property, finance and the stock market. His friends expressed great surprise, therefore, when he started talking openly about spirituality, philosophy and healing. David, though, was in for the biggest surprise of all.

Over the next few weeks, he was invited out on a series of luncheons and dinner dates by colleagues and friends, each of whom confessed a secret interest in matters spiritual. An ex-boss told David he read the book *Conversations with God* in bed every night. Another ex-boss told David he meditated and practiced Tai Chi. A lawyer friend admitted to liking Louise Hay and drinking herbal tea! One by one they confessed their closet spirituality.

People often say they are put off spirituality because they see so few stylish, strong, spiritual role models. In other words, they fear that being spiritual means you have to wear beads, speak in tongues, bible bash, eat tofu, talk to trees, like incense and have a dolphin in the bath. Of course, the real fear of spirituality is that you have to give up your cynicism, your fear, your anger and your pain. Being truly spiritual means growing up.

Without any spirituality, you are at the mercy of your ego. This is like appointing an embryo as the CEO of your life. Nothing is more terrifying than trying to play God with your own life. When you play God, there is no room for extra help, higher inspiration, true creativity or the real thing. No wonder you end up busy, self-obsessed and disconnected.

True spirituality is about connectivity, i.e., connecting to something higher than your ego. It takes you past your separate self, your physical senses, your logic and your everyday mind—to a higher ground full of inspiration and light. This is the land of miracles, eureka and divine intervention. Here is where you see that the ego is but a single slab of stone compared to the cathedral that is your higher self.

Connectivity is an inner ascension to the highest in you. It is about listening to the voice of truth within. It is when you stop listening to this voice that you lose touch with your true power and creativity. Now you rely on effort, not inspiration; on busyness, not vision; on psychology, not soul; on struggle, not surrender; on searching, not being; on fear, not love; and, on ego, not God.

True spirituality is not a quest; it is a way of being. It is about being original, i.e., connecting to original innocence, original joy, original light, original love. Your learned self is but a pale carbon copy of your true, Unconditioned Self. The French philosopher Pierre Teilhard de Chardin once wrote,

"You are not a human being who has spiritual experiences; you are a spiritual being who has human experiences."

Meditate every day. Visit the cathedral that is your higher mind. Light a candle, breathe deep, and contemplate these three questions. One, *"Did I connect well today?"* Did you go beyond your ego today? Two, *"Did I listen well today?"* Did you make way for wisdom? Did you let your soul guide you? Three, *"Did I love well today?"* Love is the *real* miracle.

LOVE IS YOUR TRUE POWER

When you stop putting love first in your life, you die a little or a lot. You live as much as you love.

Every given moment of your life you are choosing between love and something else. Love is your touchstone, your power, your true purpose. When you put love first, before everything, it inspires everything. Love is attractive, i.e., you attract great things when you love. With love you become even more creative, connected, fearless and alive—and the whole world is aroused by you.

Life works when you love; it falls apart when you don't. When you stop putting love first, you may not notice anything initially, but soon symptoms of fear and death will circle over you like vultures over a corpse. You get busy, your face hardens, you live life fast, time speeds up, you forget to smile, gratitude disappears, you get cynical, you accumulate endlessly, you are not as friendly as you once were, and you are in too much of a hurry to enjoy the moment.

Whenever you are in pain or conflict, you can be sure that you have chosen something other than love. Ask yourself, "*What have I put before love here?*" Is it money before love, career before love, mortgage and bills, fame and status, being right, your ego, protection, lies, fear?

Love comes first. There is no genuine happiness without love, no real success without love, no true peace without love, no authentic power without love, no great prosperity without love, no heartfelt wisdom without love. Have you worked this out yet? Are you putting love first?

I have a screensaver on my computer which I wrote, called *First Love*. It helps me remember. It reads:

First love, then think.
First love, then speak.
First love, then look.
First love, then act.
First love, then choose.
First love, then give.
First love, then live.

Whenever you are not loving, you lose your anchor, you have no compass, you forget what is important, life gets stormy, and relationships hit the rocks. Pain, conflict and struggle are signals to reset your course, to remember your true purpose, and to put love first again. The following questions are designed to help you stay on course.

Am I being loving, or am I searching for love? There is a world of difference between searching for love and being loving.

Am I being loving, or am I busy? What are you chasing? Are you too busy building your future to be loving right now?

Am I being loving, or am I at work? Do not separate love and work. Work is meant to be love in action. Be wholehearted at work and you will attract success.

Am I being loving, or am I trying to get something? Agendas, demands and expectations lead to pain. Unconditional love receives, but it does not take.

Am I being loving, or am I trying to win approval? Are you being authentic, or are you trying to impress, people-please, keep someone or win someone back?

Am I being loving, or am I trying to change someone? Whenever you try to change someone, fix someone, save someone, improve someone, clone someone, there will be a power struggle.

Am I being loving, or am I fighting to be right? Do you want to be right or happy? Do you want to be superior or happy? Do you want a pedestal or a partnership?

Am I being loving, or am I waiting for love? When you wait for love, it's a long wait!

Am I being loving, or am I playing it safe? You once got hurt, and now you have so many rules, boundaries and defenses that love cannot heal you.

Choose to greet this day with an open heart. Make love more important than your career today. Pour love into everything you do today. Bless and love everyone you meet today. Look on all things with appreciation and gratitude today. Make love more precious than your old wounds and old fears today. Let yourself be loved today. Make life all about love today.

LAUGHTER IS A STATE OF MIND

All my life I have toyed with the idea, *"Wouldn't it be great to be able to bottle laughter?"* I finally put my idea to the test in the summer of 1998 when I set up The Laughter Bank to collect deposits of laughter.

For three days they came—people of all ages, nationalities, religions and backgrounds. They came to donate their laugh, for free, to *The Laughter Bank*. Young babies, grandfathers, brothers and sisters, husbands and wives, mothers and sons, circles of friends and complete strangers joined together in a unique celebration of life, love and laughter.

A special sound studio was set up to record solo laughs and laughter circles, i.e., whole families, close friends, complete strangers, just children, women only, men only, different nationalities, and an interfaith circle. I was after pure, unreasonable laughter, i.e., laughter for no reason. Hence, the only stimulant available was mineral water!

Nine hours of beautiful, contagious laughter was eventually edited down to thirty minutes and published as *The Laughter*

Album. When you listen to this album, you are reminded of two great truths: 1) laughter is our universal language; 2) laughter is the best medicine. Where there is laughter, there is connection, acceptance, healing and hope.

The Laughter Album is a celebration of the true joy that exists beyond all separation, all fear, all hurt and all conflict. It affirms the universal, spiritual and infinite over all things temporal and transient. *The Laughter Album* has since made its way to all four corners of this world. It is played in hospitals, schools, healing workshops, drama schools, radio stations, car stereos and people's homes.

Laughter is victory over fear. As with love, when you forget to laugh you lose your natural, God-given immunity to fear, anxiety, ego, vanity, self-importance and over-seriousness. *You lose your way when you lose your laugh.* It is the spirit of laughter that animates acts of loving kindness, that inspires fresh hope and new resolve, that ignites your irrepressible heart, that connects you to what is true.

Laughter gives you a choice. Laughter helps you play with new perceptions, entertain novel ideas, shift your thinking, turn beliefs upside down, and exercise different options.

Laughter keeps you lateral. Hence, when you laugh you can feel fear *and* choose love; you can feel angry *and* choose peace; you can feel anxious *and* choose hope; you can be in hell *and* choose heaven.

Laughter is a let go! The joy of laughter is that you cannot laugh and hold on to pain. Laughter is like a mental shampoo that washes away old grievances, old fears, old wounds, old prejudices, old irritations. Over-seriousness blows problems up; laughter blows problems away. As the psychologist and mystic Alan Watts once wrote, "The whole art of life is in knowing how to transform anxiety into laughter."

Laughter is a medicine. It is the only medicine you can overdose on that actually helps you live even better to tell the tale! For over ten years now I have lectured to doctors, nurses, psychologists and therapists on the healing power of laughter. Mind, body and soul light up like a bright neon light whenever you laugh. Laughter promotes wellness and a happy frame of mind.

For centuries, doctors have searched high and low for a laughter organ, a laughter gland, a laughter center in the brain, a laughter hormone and even laughter DNA. No luck so far!

The origins of laughter are not physical. Laughter is a state of mind. It is a vote for love over fear, spirit over ego, mind over matter, freedom over struggle, choice over circumstance.

Laughter makes way for grace. For this reason, laughter has often been described as a form of prayer, as a song of the soul, and as God's hand on a troubled world. At its highest level, laughter transports you from your ego to the center of your Unconditioned Self where you experience a deep, deep knowing that *you are safe, whole and well.* Laughter affirms your wholeness, and it heals misperceptions of isolation, fear and weakness.

Laugh now! My very first personal letterhead carried a quote from the French philosopher, Sebastian Chamfort: "*The most wasted day is that in which we have not laughed.*" Laughter links you up to your higher self, to your heart, to your creative mind, to infinite possibilities now. Do not wait for all your problems to disappear before you laugh again. The trick is to laugh now, let go now, have fun now, dance now, smile now. Laughter transforms perception. *Laughter is victory!*

SOME OF THE BEST GIFTS
COME BADLY WRAPPED

I opened my first psychotherapy practice when I was twenty-two years old. For the first two years I had a low client base and high overheads. I struggled financially. Several times I was tempted to give up and get a "proper" job in marketing or something. One time in particular I was offered a lucrative sales job in New York but, much to my own dismay, my intuition said, "No thanks".

I remember one day receiving two letters in the mail. One was from my bank informing me that I was $900 overdrawn. The other letter was from the tax office which I left unopened because I had no money to pay yet another bill. Eventually, after a month or so, I thought I had better open the tax office letter because I didn't want to incur a late payment penalty.

When I opened the letter, I found that it wasn't a bill; it was a tax refund for $960! This was totally unexpected. What joy! And what irony! For a whole month I had struggled with no money while this lifesaving "gift" remained unopened in my in-tray. I wrote in my own personal journal that day, "Sometimes great gifts are not well wrapped. Don't let the wrapping put you off."

Things are not always what they seem. There are gifts everywhere waiting to be unwrapped. You just have to stay open. I now believe that even if that tax office letter had been a bill, another gift would have soon appeared for me. I believe in gifts. I didn't use to, but I do now, and the more I believe in gifts the more gifts I experience!

A couple of years ago I co-wrote a book on unconditional gratitude with my friend, Marika Burton, called *Everyday Is a Gift*. Unconditional gratitude is the art of being open enough to see the gift in everything. It is not just an attitude; it is a philosophy—a philosophy based on four cornerstones: 1) trust; 2) vision; 3) choice; 4) receiving.

1) *Trust*. Unconditional gratitude trusts that you live in a purposeful universe in which every experience can be used as a spur for greater happiness, wholeness and success. It is knowing that within every situation—painful or peaceful, ugly or beautiful—there is always a gift waiting for you.

Unconditional gratitude encourages you in every event, encounter and relationship to ask yourself, *"What is the gift here?"* Gifts are made of trust. When you stay open, and keep asking, gifts unwrap themselves before you.

2) *Vision.* Unconditional gratitude is essentially a training in vision. It encourages you to look not just with your eyes but also with your heart. It asks you to look again at everything you have judged as "bad", "negative" and "hopeless", and see another possibility. In truth, every problem hides a gift. When you look for gifts, gifts appear.

It is a good habit to ask yourself in any situation, *"What shall I see here?"* What will you focus on? Remember, perception is a choice. You can also ask yourself, *"What would my best friend see here?"* Or, *"What would the person I most respect see here?"* Or, *"What would Jesus see here?"* (or Buddha, or God, etc.) Unconditional gratitude helps you look at all things with open-mindedness.

3) *Choice.* Unconditional gratitude is knowing that you have the power to choose your life. In every moment you are choosing what you want. For instance, you may be choosing between staying open or closing down, being present or living in the past, letting go or holding on, taking responsibility or blaming, asking for help or not, trying something new or not.

You can choose your life, and you can choose your response

to any circumstance in your life. Ask yourself then, "*What do I want here?*" What is your intention? Where will you place your energy? What will you say "Yes" to?

4) *Receiving.* Give up your judgments, lay aside your fears and look beyond all appearances for the gift that awaits you. Hold a space in your mind for the possibility of blessings in every situation. Be willing to receive. Affirm how well you want to receive today.

In the English language, the word "present" has three distinct meanings: "here", "now" and "a gift". Wherever you are, there is a gift waiting for you. Sometimes gifts come wrapped in loss, pain, failure, fear and tears, but, remember, *the gift is not the wrapping.*

STAY OPEN ALL HOURS
FOR MIRACLES

Today is just a normal day full of miracles,
gifts and opportunities.

I shall never forget the day my brother-in-law, Josh, and I went on a chartered deep-sea fishing trip off the coast of Perth, Australia. The trip was a gift from my father-in-law, Grant. It was my first time deep-sea fishing, and both Josh and I had high hopes. We told the family there would definitely be fish for dinner.

For two hours the charter boat powered its way out to sea beating off big waves and high winds. It was not long before I was hanging my head over the side being violently sick. Of the twenty crew on board that day, only two did not get seasick—the captain and his dog.

When the shoreline finally disappeared, the captain cut the engines and issued rods, bait and harnesses. Several people caught good-sized fish with their first casts. We were a little disappointed, therefore, when our first attempt failed. Three hours later, we were the only ones not to have caught anything. Nothing. Not even a bite. No luck at all.

After six hours we were wet, tired, dehydrated, sunburned, seasick, covered in fish bait and still without a fish. But we kept on casting off and we kept on *giving up*, i.e., we gave up our disappointment, our frustration, our sense of failure and the temptation to stop. We told jokes, caught imaginary fish, made up songs, and kept casting *as if for the first time*. We reasoned that if our lines were in the sea we still had hope.

Finally, after eight hours, the captain signaled it was time to head for land. "Just one more go," I pleaded.

"But you've got no more bait," the captain said.

"We're feeling lucky," said Josh. The captain gave way, and we cast off one last time—with no bait. Instantly I felt a tug. At first I thought I imagined it. Together we reeled in a beautiful twenty-pound Queensland Snapper—the biggest catch of the day.

A thousand times I have used this story to remind myself to stay open all hours for miracles.

If you are like everyone else on this planet, you have been tempted a thousand times to give up on life, love, happiness and yourself. You have experienced failure, heartbreak, pain and personal hell. It is one of the world's worst kept secrets that everyone—yes, everyone—has had a dark night of the soul. We have all wanted to give up and die.

When life is not working for you, you are being asked to *give up*. Yes! You are being asked to give up thoughts, beliefs, perceptions, habits and fears that hold you back. There can be no new miracles whilst you are holding on to the old stuff. Pain is a signal to let go, give something up, open up and try something new.

Whenever you are stuck, out of luck, on your knees or tempted to give up hope, ask yourself, "*What am I being asked to give up?*" What is holding you back? Read the following list slowly. Let your higher mind answer intuitively "Yes" or "No" as you ask yourself, *am I being asked to give up* …

- addiction to struggle
- trying too hard
- lack of faith in life
- unworthiness
- self-doubt
- cynicism
- disbelief

- expectations and plans
- dysfunctional independence
- unhealthy competitiveness
- playing small
- patterns of sacrifice
- fear of rejection
- an old disappointment
- an old wound
- an old heartbreak
- an old mistake
- an old fear
- bitterness at my ex-partner
- resentment at my mother
- anger at my father
- fury at God
- fear of happiness
- fear of success
- fear of love
- fear of abundance
- fear of wellness

"*I give up*" is a good place to be when you are willing to let go of what is not working for you. When you give up you can put your mind in God's hands and cynicism can make way for hope, worry can make way for inspiration, disappointment can make way for adventure, and the old can make way for something new and better. This is how miracles happen.

Ask yourself, *"Shall I live by memory or imagination today?"* Today is brand-new. You have not "done" today before. Be wide open for miracles. Think to yourself, *"Now is new."* Give up the old. Allow yourself to be open to a new vision, a new way of thinking and a new way of living. Every moment invites you to begin again.

GET OFF YOUR "YEAH, BUT"

Making changes for the better requires a small helping of "how to" and a large helping of "want to". Willingness is the key.

In my *Shift Happens!* seminars I often use a perception test called "Nine Dots" (see below). The goal is to connect the nine dots using four straight lines *without* taking your pen off the page. Have a go. The answer is at the end of this chapter.

Four lines is enough. You do not need more resources. With real life challenges the initial temptation often is to call for more resources (i.e., more learning, more skills, more wisdom, more support, more opportunity). The way to succeed with "Nine Dots"—and most real challenges—is to think differently, i.e., to "step out of the box".

I use "Nine Dots" as an introduction to talking about "the box". Life is all about falling into the box and finding your way out again.

The box is a symbol for your ego. It represents your conditioning, old thinking, learned self-doubts, self-imposed limits and imagined thresholds of success, happiness and love. The box is what is familiar to you. It is life *as you define it*. The walls of the box are made of fear, and thus are not really real. To venture beyond the box takes nothing special other than courage and willingness.

Beyond the box is your Unconditioned Self—a new world full of new stories and new possibilities. Here is where you remember boundless bliss, ecstatic creativity, immeasurable peace and joy unlimited. To step out of the box you have to be willing to drop the past, laugh off your fears, let go of old wounds, unlearn your beliefs, look with new eyes and try something new.

Are you ready to step out of the box? Are you ready to be free again?

I once observed in a psychology class a science experiment about a swarm of fruit flies housed in a special clear plexiglas box. The wings of the fruit flies were so delicate that if they touched the plexiglas they would die. Very quickly they learned to fly within the parameters of the box. The scientists then removed the walls of the box, leaving the fruit flies free to go, but instead they continued to hover in the same spot until they died.

Are you flying free? Are you alive, spontaneous and open to all that is really possible? Or are you renting a box?

To step out of the box, you have to question what you have taught yourself about life. A good question to ask yourself is, "*What is my truth?*", or "*What am I trying to make real?*" For instance, what is your philosophy about happiness? What beliefs do you have about love? What "laws" have you decreed about money and abundance? What self-made limits do you observe about success? What is your reality?

Sitting in your box, you constantly talk yourself out of the good things in life, i.e., you want to say "Yes" but you end up on "Yeah, but"! With "Yeah, but" you "try" to say "Yes" but ultimately you never get past "No", "Can't", "But", "What if",

"Not now" and "Shouldn't". Courage and willingness will get you out of your box.

Imagine what stepping out of the box would look like in your relationships. Notice any fears, and feel what joy you would experience. Imagine what stepping out of the box would look like in your work. Notice any fears, and feel the success you would enjoy. Imagine what stepping out of the box would look like in your life overall. Notice any fears, and keep feeling all the possibilities that emerge.

You cannot shift your life and sit on your "Yeah, but". "Yeah, but" won't make you happy and it can't keep you safe; in fact it can only give you blisters! Sitting in one place for long enough does that! "Yeah, but" is fear. It is a thousand excuses for sticking with the same-old, same-old. Ultimately, "Yeah, but" is resistance to joy. You are all boxed up with nowhere to go.

One way to get off your "Yeah, but" and really step out of the box is to start practicing the end of fear. Every day, take a few moments to meditate on fearlessness. Imagine what your life could really be like if you let go of fear, separation, ego, limits, conditions, rules, laws, reasons, musts, oughts, shoulds, everything. This might be frightening at first, but if you stick with it you will eventually rediscover your Unconditioned Self.

In truth, there is no box and there are no limits. Meditating on fearlessness will help you remember this.

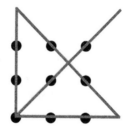

YOUR HAPPINESS IS A GIFT

There is an old saying, *some people grow up and spread cheer, others just grow up and spread!* You are a gift. You have a gift for everyone who is in your life, and they have a gift for you too. You would not meet otherwise.

In August 1996, the BBC broadcast a forty-minute documentary on my work entitled *How to be Happy*. It has since been broadcast in sixteen countries to over 30 million television viewers. The documentary assembled a team of independent scientists to test if it really is possible for people to choose happiness. My eight-week happiness course, called *Happiness NOW!*, was chosen as the focus model.

Caroline was one of three volunteers chosen for the documentary. Her application read, "Middle-aged, depressed, isolated and searching for happiness". Six years before she had given up her full-time job to care for her invalid mother. "I know I did the right thing, but now I feel lost and lonely. I would love to feel as if I have something to offer somebody again," she wrote.

Caroline and the other volunteers were tested for "happiness levels" during my eight-week course and for a further six months afterwards, using two well respected psychometric tests—the Oxford Happiness Inventory and the Otago University Affectometer. For "harder" evidence, Caroline was flown to Madison University, Wisconsin for biofeedback tests measuring neurochemistry and brainwave function.

Viewers watched on as all three volunteers made remarkable breakthroughs over the next few weeks. When Caroline returned to Wisconsin for her final tests, the scientists observed, "Caroline's brain function had shifted so much that the Madison University computer could not plot her increased happiness on the standard graph." The Head Professor said, "*What these results show is that the happiness training not only changed the way you feel; it has actually changed the way your brain functions.*"

Caroline's transformation made her a household heroine overnight. Her courage to heal and be happy was a gift to millions. For the next two years people everywhere asked me to pass on their heartfelt thanks to Caroline. I also remember one time when Caroline had to cut short our telephone counseling session because a Canadian radio station wanted her to "go live" with her top ten secrets for happiness!

Helen Keller wrote, "Although the world is very full of suffering, it is also full of the overcoming of it." In other words, shift happens! Caroline discovered a great gift and a new purpose when she accepted healing and happiness for herself. The whole world gains when one person has the courage to heal, to love and to be happy. No one is healed alone.

You are a gift-bearer. You are the "light of the world", and so is the person next to you. Do not forget your purpose. Do not be distracted with "getting" and "having" and "to-ing" and "fro-ing". Do not give in to fear and do not let old wounds blow you off course. Your healing is a gift. Your happiness is a gift. Your loving touch is a gift. Give yourself, heart and soul, and find out who you really are.

You are gift-wrapped.
Unwrap yourself now.
Let your gifts spill to the floor
and all over the world.

Watch how your kindness
transforms this cruel world.
See how your love heals fear.

SHIFT HAPPENS!

Notice how your courage
inspires us all.

Let your smile release
this sad old world.
Give everyone you meet
the star in your eye.
Shine your light.
Open your heart.

Notice how your peace of
mind makes any war more
meaningless and harder
to fight.

Your happiness is a gift.
It attracts angels from afar.
Your smile is like champagne.
Your laughter is like love.
Your healing inspires us.
Your Presence is a miracle.
Unwrap yourself now.

FURTHER INFORMATION

ROBERT HOLDEN Ph.D. is the Director of The Happiness Project —a pioneer in the field of positive psychology and well-being. His innovative work on the psychology of happiness has been the subject of two BBC documentaries including, "*How to Be Happy*"—now shown in 16 countries to over 30 million TV viewers. For further information on this work visit the website: www.happiness.co.uk.

Robert is also the Director of Success Intelligence. He has designed and delivered major seminars to thousands of professionals over the years. His clients include the BBC, Coca Cola, KPMG, The Body Shop, Sony Corporation and Marriott Hotels. He has also personally coached the Directors of many Fortune 500 companies. For further information on this work visit the website: www.successintelligence.com

SHIFT HAPPENS! LIBRARY

The following list of books and tapes are recommended for personal alchemy and inner transformation:

A Course in Miracles. Viking Adult, 1996

Berke, Diane. *Love Always Answers.* Crossroads, 1994;
  The Gentle Smile. Crossroads, 1994

Carlson, Richard. *Don't Sweat The Small Stuff!* Hyperion, 1997

Carpenter, Tom. *Dialogue on Awakening.* Carpenter Press, 1992

Chopra, Deepak. *The Seven Spiritual Laws of Success.* New
  World Library, 1994

Cohen, Alan. *A Deep Breath of Life.* Hay House, 1996

Frankl, Victor. *Man's Search for Meaning.* Washington Square
  Press, 1984

Fromm, Erich. *The Art of Loving.* Harper Perennial, 2000;
  To Have or To Be? Continuum International, 1996

Gangaji. *The Diamond in Your Pocket.* Sounds True, 2005

Holden, Robert. *Happiness NOW!* Hodder & Stoughton, 1998; *Hello Happiness.* Hodder & Stoughton, 1999; *Success Intelligence.* Hodder & Stoughton, 2005

Holden, Miranda. *Boundless Love.* Rider & Co, 2002

Huber, Cheri. *There is Nothing Wrong With You.* Keep It Simple Books, 2001

Jampolsky, Gerald. *Love is Letting Go of Fear.* Celestial Arts, 1984

Jeffers, Susan. *Feel The Fear And Do It Anyway.* Fawcett Ballantine, 1988; *Life is Huge!.* Jeffers Press, 2005; *The Feel the Fear Guide to Lasting Love.* Jeffers Press, 2005

Katie, Byron. *Loving What Is.* Three Rivers Press, 2003; *I Need Your Love—Is That True?* Harmony, 2005

Mundy, Jon. *Awaken to Your Own Call.* Crossroads, 1994

Poonja, H.W.L. *Wake Up and Roar Vol 1.* Gangaji Foundation, 1992; *Wake Up and Roar Vol 2.* Gangaji Foundation, 1993

Renshaw, Ben. *Successful but Something Missing!* Rider & Co, 2000

Riso, Don & Hudson, Russ. *The Wisdom of the Enneagram.* Bantam, 1999

Roman, Sanaya. *Living With Joy.* H.J. Kramer. 1986

Spezzano, Chuck. *If it Hurts, it isn't Love.* Marlowe & Co, 2000; *Heal Your Heartbreak*, Marlowe & Co, 2001

Spezzano, Lency. *Make Way for Love.* Psychology of Vision Press, 2000

Williams, Nick. *The Work We Were Born To Do*. Element, 2000